BEAUTY GUIDE

Muscle Contraction Treatment

Beauty Guides by Ann Gallant
1. Muscle Contraction Treatment
2. Figure Treatment
3. Galvanic Treatment
4. Epilation Treatment

Also by Stanley Thornes (Publishers) Ltd

Joyce Allsworth	*Skin Camouflage: A Guide to Remedial Techniques*
Elaine Almond	*Safety in the Salon*
W E Arnould-Taylor	*The Principles and Practice of Physical Therapy*
W E Arnould-Taylor	*Aromatherapy for the Whole Person*
Ann Gallant	*Body Treatments and Dietetics for the Beauty Therapist*
Ann Gallant	*Principles and Techniques for the Electrologist*
Ann Gallant	*Principles and Techniques for the Beauty Specialist*
Ann Hagman	*The Aestheticienne*
John Rounce	*Science for the Beauty Therapist*

BEAUTY GUIDE 1

Muscle Contraction Treatment

Ann Gallant

F.S.H.B.Th., Int.B.Th.Dip., D.R.E. (Tutor),
Teacher's Certificate in Further Education

*Formerly Lecturer Responsible
for Beauty Therapy at
Chichester College of Higher Technology, and
Gloucestershire College of Art and Technology*

Stanley Thornes (Publishers) Ltd

© Ann Gallant 1985

All rights reserved. No part of this publication may be reproduced, stored in a retrieval system or transmitted in any form or by any means, electronic, mechanical, recording or otherwise, without the prior written consent of the copyright holders. Applications for such permission should be addressed to the publishers: Stanley Thornes (Publishers) Ltd, Old Station Drive, Leckhampton, CHELTENHAM GL53 0DN, England.

First published in 1985 by
Stanley Thornes (Publishers) Ltd,
Old Station Drive,
Leckhampton,
CHELTENHAM GL53 0DN

British Library Cataloguing in Publication Data

Gallant, Ann
   Muscle contraction treatment.—(Beauty guides; 1)
   1. Beauty, Personal
   I. Title   II. Series
   646.7'2   RA778

ISBN 0-85950-213-9

Typeset in 10/11 Garamond
by Tech-Set, Gateshead, Tyne & Wear.
Printed and bound in Great Britain
at The Bath Press, Avon.

Contents

Chapter 1	The Faradic System	1
Chapter 2	How Muscle Contraction Works	7
Chapter 3	Suitability of Treatment	14
Chapter 4	Practical Points	22
Chapter 5	Principles of Faradic Padding	24
Chapter 6	Applying Muscle Toning Treatment	42
Chapter 7	Facial Faradism	55
Useful Addresses		66

Acknowledgements

My thanks go to my husband, Robin Cleugh, who worked with patience and skill to provide all the photographs in this practical guide — making it so much more usable to the beauty practitioner working in the field. Thanks also to Angela Lumley for her care in the line drawings and sympathetic approach to the subject. For my daughter Patsy's forbearance in acting as a model for the photographs, I'd like to record a special mother's appreciation.

1

The faradic system

INTRODUCTION TO MUSCLE CONTRACTION

One of the most popular methods of figure shaping for the client is muscle contraction or passive exercise, because it does not involve much personal effort and yet is very effective. Certainly, muscle contraction treatment through *faradism* is a valuable and profitable part of salon work.

It is at its best when offered as part of a combined programme of treatment. Saunas, steam baths, jacuzzis (hydrotherapy whirlpools) and impulse showers all act as good pre-heating preparations before reduction and specific muscle toning treatments. These improve the results achieved and offer the client a pleasant and comfortable treatment.

Muscle contraction uses faradic-type currents to artificially stimulate and exercise the muscles, and improve vascular and lymphatic circulation responses in the area of treatment. As with natural exercise, when the muscles are made to work, associated systems work too, improving their function. *So muscles can be strengthened, or shortened, as they improve in tone, or even built up very slowly by muscle contraction.* Thus it is important for the *purpose* of the application to be known when working out a treatment plan. Muscles may need shortening and tightening (contracting along their length or long axis), and this requires a different approach to strengthening or building up muscles (resulting in an increase in muscle bulk). So figures can not only be reshaped with muscle contraction, they can also be improved.

MUSCLE CONTRACTION SYSTEMS — FARADIC TYPE

The *Beauty Gallery* ten outlet (20 pad) faradic system of muscle contraction provides a wide range of treatment opportunities, and gives comfortable surged contractions very similar to those experienced during natural exercise. The smoothness of the current flow gives a rounded feeling *contraction* and *release,* which is very acceptable to the client.

THE 'BEAUTY GALLERY' WITH ITS FARADIC MUSCLE CONTRACTION AND BODY GALVANIC CELLULITE SYSTEMS

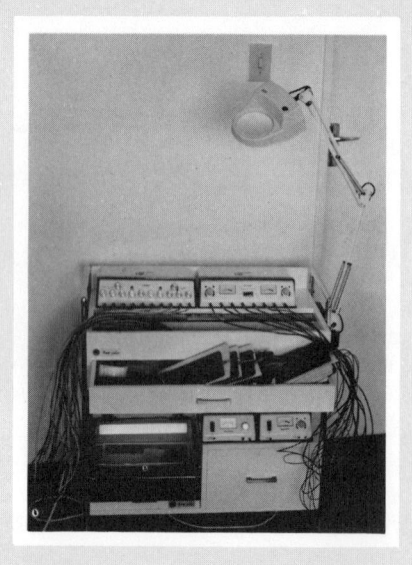

The pulse or contraction rate has been professionally set to perform effective, comfortable exercise of the muscles, and for most purposes can be left in the 'normal' position. A pulse light indicates the actual contraction rate.

The faster pulse provides more contractions per minute and limits their effect. The slower pulse provides fewer contractions in the same period, but they are sustained or held fractionally longer. All the contraction rates are very close to natural exercise, and so the client's preference as to 'feel' should be followed.

Each of the system's ten outlets can be individually controlled for intensity, and the conductive pads allow a comfortable flow of current which cuts down initial prickling and provides contractions at a low level of intensity. Each pair of pads alternates for polarity, changing frequently from negative to positive, positive to negative, so the contraction formed is very regular, with the muscle contracting naturally, becoming bulkier on each stimulus. A contraction which causes the two ends of the muscle to come closer together is termed a contraction along the *long axis* or *length of the muscle*.

Polarity as such is not important, as muscles are not, by nature, confined to pull only one way, but rather to contract and become more bulky or firm as the muscle stimulation occurs. Artifical muscle contraction aims to copy natural action, and works the muscle as it would perform in life, just as if it was working under normal nervous stimulation from the brain, with conscious control. The *Beauty Gallery* faradic system provides ample outlets for group pad placings, so that different areas of the body needing varying levels of current intensity can be treated, as all the outlets have individual controls.

'BEAUTY GALLERY' UNIT COMPLETE WITH FARADIC SYSTEM

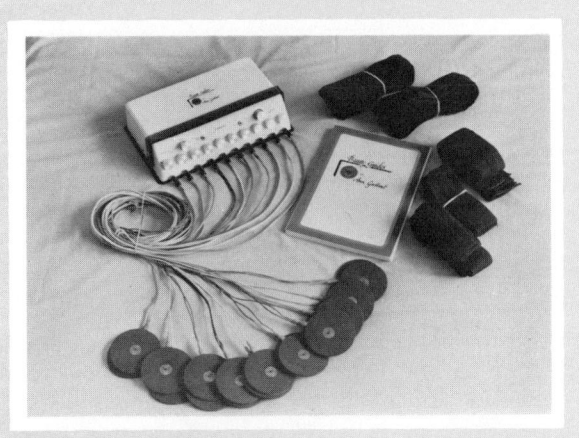

(a) The faradic system:
ten outlet (20 pad),
body straps (14),
guide to muscle contraction.
Moulded pads have conductive working surfaces and non-conductive backs (engraved) for safety

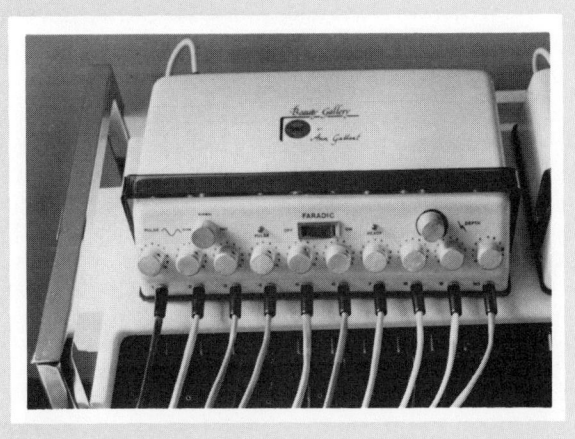

(b) The faradic unit:
ten outlets, individually controlled,
'on/off' and 'pulse' control,
'depth' control,
'ready' light,
'pulse' light

SAFETY FEATURES

To avoid commencing treatment with any intensity control knobs in the active working position, a special safety feature has been built into the *Beauty Gallery* faradic system. Until all outlet controls are at zero, the 'ready' light will not come on, and the controls will not operate. This warns the operator that an outlet control knob has been left in the active intensity position, and must be corrected. Once all numbered knobs are at zero, *and the machine is switched off and on again,* the ready light comes on, and all the system's controls are ready for use.

IMPROVED COMFORT FREQUENCY

In the latest machines a small amount of anaesthetic current is built into the frequency, which dramatically improves client comfort. This slight deadening effect overcomes the superficial prickling under the pads at low levels of intensity, and provides easy, comfortable contractions at much lower levels of current. This major technical advance in muscle contraction applications allows a much greater range of clients to benefit from treatment, and reduces anxiety in the treatment application. Without the primary reaction in the skin, the motor point of the muscle can be far more easily stimulated, and active contractions will occur at low levels of current intensity. This improved comfort facility should be demanded in all new muscle contraction equipment, for the client's benefit in treatment, as it is a real technical breakthrough for the industry.

DEPTH CONTROL

The 'depth' control provides a means of increasing the muscle contraction's effect deep into the tissues, by changing the frequency pattern slightly. It affects all the outlets in use in an equal way, and can be used when the client has a lot of subcutaneous fat overlying the muscles, or where a stronger overall effect is needed for some reason, perhaps because the client suffers from extremely weak muscle tone.

It is an easy way to increase equally the total effect but should only be used when the client has become accustomed to the contractions, has settled into them, and muscle activity has reduced. A very small increase in the depth control brings all areas back to an active working level. If only certain individual areas need increased effect and others are working satisfactorily, then these increases should be controlled on the individual outlet controls for the areas.

Very weak muscles can sometimes work better on a moderate intensity level on individual outlet controls, and a moderate level of depth control. Practice will show the usefulness of the depth control and where it can be used to advantage. Its main advantage is speedy control of overall intensity, which saves the therapist a lot of time in treatment, especially when she is supervising several clients undergoing muscle contraction.

SIMPLE AND EFFECTIVE CONTROLS

The faradic system is designed in such a way that the controls are simple and effective. The operator can concentrate on client care, accurate padding, etc., knowing the machine has been expertly designed and professionally set to provide the easiest and safest system of muscle contraction. This also ensures that errors cannot occur from an inaccurate or incorrect combination of frequencies, pulse rates, polarities, etc., which could distress or harm the client causing her to lose confidence in the treatment.

COLOUR-CODED LEADS

To aid the therapist in her task of fast and accurate padding up, the connection leads are colour-coded so that any pads found to need repositioning, or requiring changes in intensity, or thought to be causing discomfort, can be quickly identified and the problem dealt with. The colour coding is also useful when areas of the body need to have their intensities increased gradually to obtain or maintain an active contraction level. Then there is no danger of the intensity being increased to the wrong muscles, as the leads can simply be traced by looking at the colour leads connected to the active pads, and matching this colour on the lead as it connects into the machine. With group paddings, where many pads are positioned in a small area, this is a very useful point in the application.

PADDING UP
Accurate placing of pads plus neat and firm strapping is vital for good results

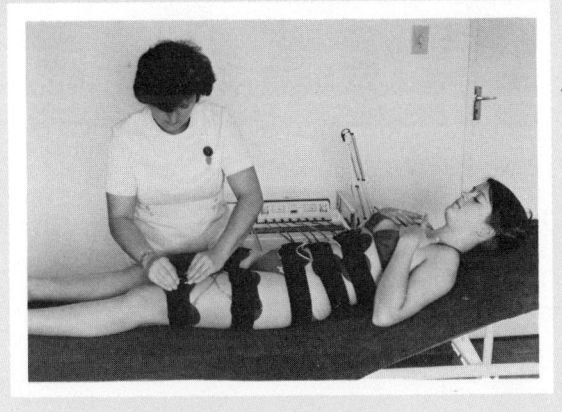

ADJUSTING THE PADS
With colour-coded leads, pads needing adjustments during treatment can quickly be identified

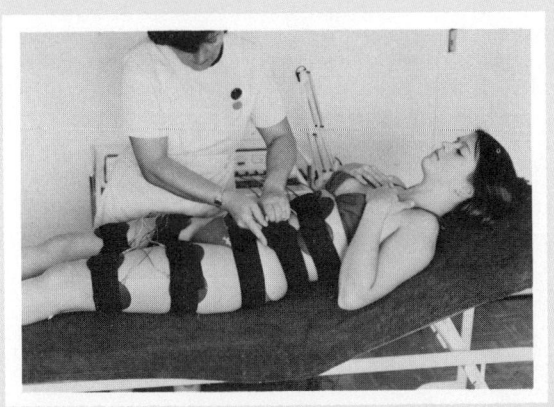

The colour-coded leads are covered along part of their length with clear plastic tubing to prevent tangling and for added strength. This helps to reduce preparation time, resulting in a greater earning capacity for the system. It also saves a lot of annoyance to the therapist's nerves if she does not have to keep stopping to sort out tangled leads and pads.

If the faradic system is used with the *Beauty Gallery* storage system, its pads and connection leads can be placed in the storage trays provided, and the strapping stored in the drawers making a neat and complete unit ready for immediate use anywhere in the clinic or health centre.

REMOVING THE PADS

As pads are removed, their clear sleeving is slipped back along the leads towards the pads to prevent tangling, and they are placed in order in the storage area on the Beauty Gallery *system. Place backs to fronts to keep conductive surfaces apart and to avoid fusing the machine if power should be switched on in error*

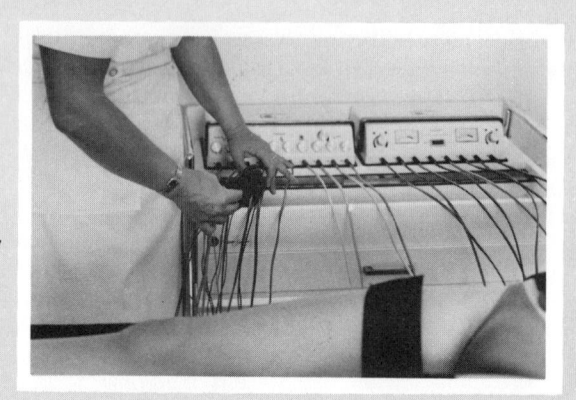

FIRM STRAPPING

Strapping the pads so that they form excellent skin contact is extremely important, so a full set of body straps is provided (14 straps) with the faradic system. These include two 60 cm long straps for the knees or arms, eight 80 cm long straps for the legs or trunk, and two 100 cm and two 120 cm long straps for full hips or buttocks or the larger client's needs. Colour badges show strap size.

These straps provide firm but comfortable support, and hold the pads securely against the body allowing the conductive material to make full contact with the skin. Generous use of Velcro zipping strips makes it possible to use the straps on a wide range of differently-sized clients, and to interchange their use. It is preferable to overstrap rather than understrap and have pads which do not make good contact, rolling up at the edges, etc. This could cause discomfort from skin prickling, primary skin reactions, etc., as the current attempts to reach and pass through the skin, so it must be avoided. Faradic burns can occur if the pads are not firmly applied to the skin, so care must be taken over this point.

Most important of all, if the padding is well placed and firmly strapped, the treatment will be much more effective and comfortable for the client.

2

How muscle contraction works

Muscle contraction systems use medium to low frequency currents which are based on the original principle of faradism (the current obtained from a faradic coil). These currents are known as faradic-type currents, and give a mixture of frequencies to improve client comfort.

The faradic system provides smooth contractions where the current is surged or interrupted so that the action closely resembles natural exercise. This surge or interruption is the pulse of the unit, and shows the amount of contractions applied in a period. This action trains the client's muscles to respond and encourages client participation in home and clinic exercise programmes to reinforce the electrical work.

If the client is extremely overweight, or the muscles are very weak, perhaps after pregnancy, injury, surgery or as a result of habitual (long term) posture faults, then muscle contraction is an excellent aid to retraining the muscles to work. The client feels an immediate response and is encouraged.

With the latest muscle contraction units, the muscle activity builds up in a smooth manner, produces a clear contraction, and releases the contraction steadily. So the contraction feels rounded at its peak, and does not feel spasmodic or sharp as it is released. The mixture of currents chosen smooths off the sharp peaks of the faradic current giving greater comfort, and stops the sharp 'grabbing' and 'letting go' sensation often experienced and disliked by clients. This smoothness and steady build of the contraction into an active visible exercise when sufficient current is used, improves the sensation the client experiences.

The active conductive pads allow the current to flow across to the *motor points* of the muscles, and only need to be moistened on their working contact surface before application. The pads' conductivity comes from an element moulded into the pads in their manufacture, and makes moist sponge coverings unnecessary and obsolete. The pads only need to be kept clean, washed and wiped over after each client with a dilute antiseptic solution (such as Milton), to prevent the build up of body oils on the pads. The pads do not need to be removed from their connection leads for cleaning, but can simply be wiped as they are sorted out and placed back in sequence in the storage tray on the *Beauty Gallery* unit. Then they are clean and ready for immediate use and have no chance to get untidy. Place pads backs to fronts only on trolley.

PRINCIPLES OF MUSCLE CONTRACTION

The basic principle of muscle contraction is to copy natural muscle movements, so that muscles increase in tone, become stronger and more able to hold contours effectively and without strain. The aim is to establish clear nerve paths and to exercise the muscles, either in groups for general toning of contours and reduction of inches/cm or specifically (in isolation) for improvement of a problem area, such as the inside thigh, inside upper arm, breasts and lower abdomen after pregnancy, the action being to tighten, flatten, or firm the area involved.

If general toning is required, a group or area placing of pads (electrodes) is used. They are placed in pairs, and work with alternating polarity, so the entire area involved is activated. When sufficient current is applied, contractions will occur if the placing has been accurate. This achieves the same results as a period of active exercise but is more specific, as associated muscles are less involved than they would be with natural exercise. This means that the weak muscle is made to work for itself; it cannot be carried by the action of stronger muscles around it.

As the effects of accurate muscle contraction are so concentrated, it is not necessary to work for very long on any one area. Really weak muscles should never be exercised for more than *10 minutes* specifically, as this is equivalent to a much longer period of natural exercise. As muscles strengthen, the timing of the application can be adjusted.

MUSCLE FATIGUE

In some cases where there are weak or disused muscles, fatigue can be seen within 10 minutes of starting contractions, and the treatment should be stopped. When unwilling muscles are being made to work, they tire very easily and may require maximum current intensity to get a response. Here the depth control can be valuable to help the muscles respond. As the muscles strengthen, less current is needed to activate them and this gives a guide to the client's general progress.

Muscle fatigue is recognized by the muscles' unwillingness to continue to respond to the electrical stimulation, and by shaking, tremors and erratic contractions. If these signs are ignored, the muscles stop responding altogether and this could result in aching, sore muscles after treatment. In treatments where the client is padded up and left without any supervision, the muscles can become fatigued without anyone realizing what is happening. Most muscle toning routines can be completed within a half-hour period — setting up and padding, application, removal, etc. — and this approach plus at least periodic checking will prevent muscle fatigue occurring.

FOLLOWING NATURAL MOVEMENTS

The natural movement of the muscles should be considered and pads placed to copy these movements as closely as possible. For example, if the muscles of an area normally work together to produce a movement, they should be padded and made to work together with artificial muscle toning. The four-part (quad) muscle of the front thigh, commonly known as the *quadriceps,* should be exercised as a group as it is not natural for each segment to work independently. The muscles of the abdominal area also have a joint role of holding in the abdominal contents, and these too can be made to work naturally in supporting each other in a group padding covering the rectus abdominis and external/internal oblique muscles. If, however, the rectus abdominis muscle is overstretched, perhaps as a result of pregnancy, then this can be exercised specifically to shorten it along its long axis (along its length from end to end). This will act to pull in the area, flatten the abdominal contents, and prevent protrusion in this weak area.

The purpose of the exercise, the state of the muscles, and the accuracy of the pad placing are all vital points in successful treatment.

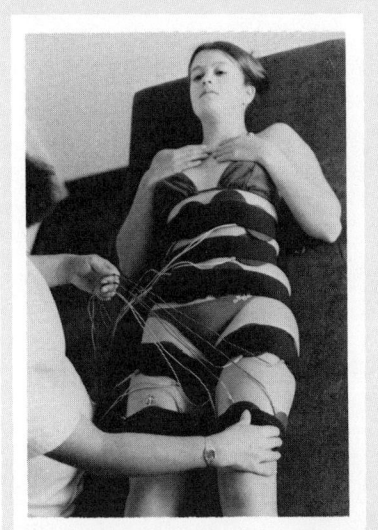

METHODS OF PLACING THE PADS

(a) Muscles work most clearly and comfortably when padded along their length, even when a general placing is applied, and multiple pads used

ACCURACY OF PAD PLACING

For either group placing or individual pointing (contraction) of muscles, an excellent knowledge of the superficial muscles of the body is essential, and *always* forms the basis for the padding layouts. Knowledge of anatomy overrides any pad placing plans which can only act as suggestions to correct padding up.

(b) An example of long axis padding on the quadriceps muscle of the thigh (along its length)

The *state* or *tone* of each client's muscles, dictates or indicates the best way to apply and perform the treatment. By using the position of the muscles in relation to their bone attachments, it is always possible to tell where the muscles are, regardless of the client's weight or size. The bones can be thought of as tent poles in the body, they stick out in strategic places and guide the operator as to the position of the muscles, and their active motor point areas.

(c) A diagonal pad placing on the thigh, where the whole area becomes suffused with current intensity and works together. Motor point accuracy is still vital, but pads are not paired along the muscle's length

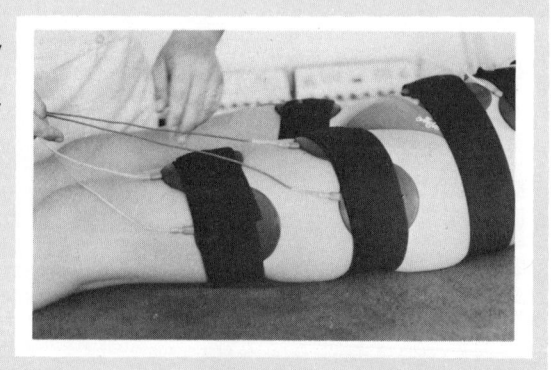

Accuracy is vital in muscle contraction work; unless the pad is placed on a motor point area, the current cannot flow along the nerve path to cause a clear and comfortable contraction. Also the primary prickling skin reaction will cause the client discomfort; since the current will always try to run towards the nerve path, a lot of current seepage and subsequent skin irritation occurs in the attempt. A lot of the discomfort associated with faradic muscle contraction comes from this inaccuracy of padding, and a lack of attention to the position of muscles and their active motor points.

HOW MUSCLES WORK

For success in all forms of muscle contraction it is necessary to study the body's muscular and skeletal systems in detail, to understand how, with the nervous system, they combine to form movement.

A study of movement (kinesiology) shows how muscles work to achieve and maintain locomotion (active movement). Muscles can work *isotonically,* that is actively with contractions causing joint movements and changes in the position of the bony skeleton. Normal active movements are of this type. The muscles can also contract *isometrically* without a change in their length, that is they do not cause joint movement, body activity, or locomotion. Artificial muscle contraction is mainly of the isometric type, muscles become thicker and bulkier between their attachment points, but do not normally cause joints to be involved. In muscle toning routines, however, if the contractions are active and effective in some areas of the body, they do affect the joint and cause movement there. One example is the large muscle group of the front thigh, which moves the knee joint actively if the pads are placed too closely to the knee itself. Also if the gastrocnemius muscle of the calf is worked actively, it causes strong downward movements of the foot, as would be the case if the movement was a natural one, a conscious action from the person.

Why this level of movement is possible with artificial exercise can be understood if it is known that muscles work by contracting towards their origin, that is their fixed point. Muscles cannot push, only pull. When the insertion, the mobile end of the muscle, and the origin, the fixed or static attachment of the muscle, come closer together, the muscle shortens on its long axis (along its length), and movement occurs at connecting joints. So artificial muscle contraction can be like natural exercise, though as it does not have the respiratory and circulatory advantages of real exercise, it should always be thought of as a reinforcement to active isotonic exercise, rather than a replacement for it.

MOTOR POINTS OF MUSCLES

Every muscle, unless deeply covered by other muscles, possesses the capacity to be exercised artificially on its motor point area. This is the area which permits the clearest contraction with the minimum amount of current used, and it is where the nerve supply to the muscle enters the bulk of the muscle. Muscles of similar shapes have their motor point in a similar position, that is a position in relation to the muscle's bony attachments, sometimes where the tendon of the muscle's origin attachment spreads to form the bulk of the muscle. Irregular muscles have no such easy

MOTOR POINTS FOR ACTIVE CONTRACTIONS

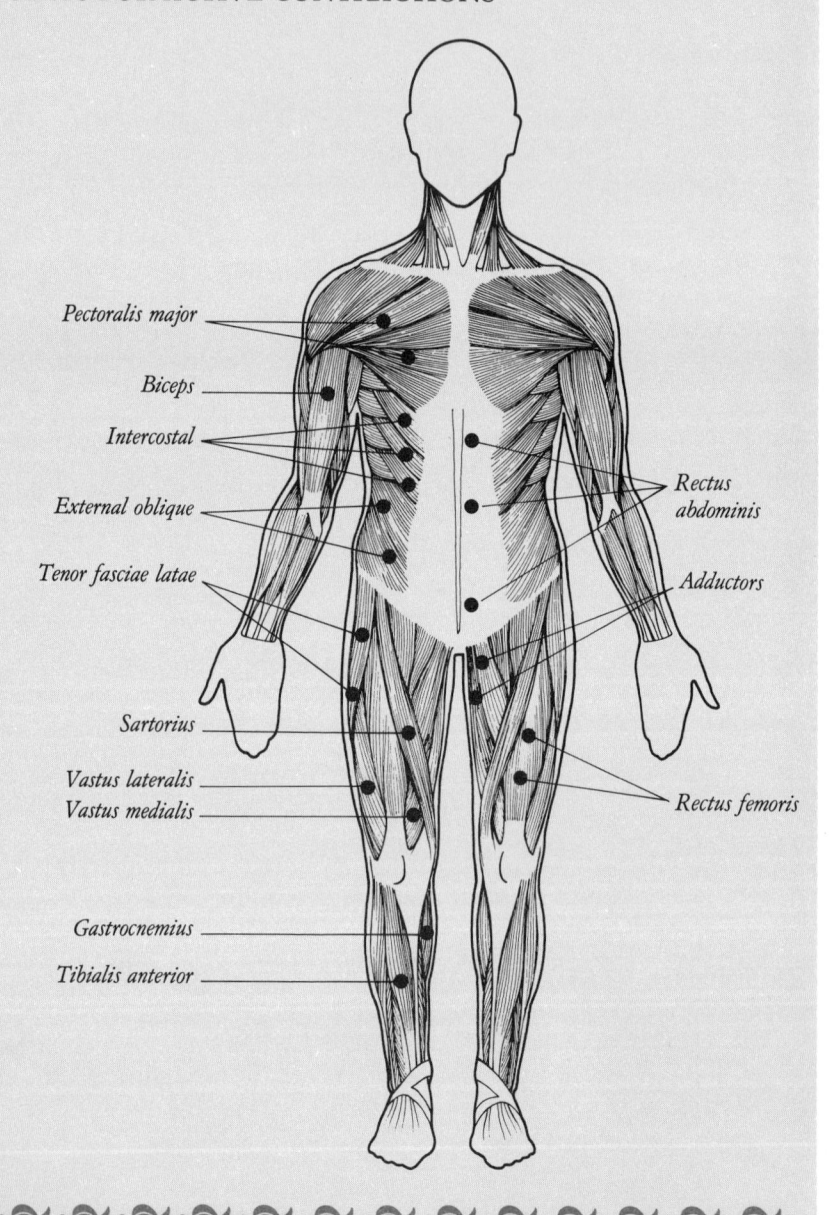

Pectoralis major

Biceps

Intercostal

External oblique

Tenor fasciae latae

Sartorius

Vastus lateralis
Vastus medialis

Gastrocnemius
Tibialis anterior

Rectus abdominis

Adductors

Rectus femoris

pattern to follow, and their motor points simply have to be learnt. Whatever the padding layout, these motor points remain of the greatest overall importance, and if they are not covered by the conductive pads, active and comfortable contractions will not be possible.

MOTOR POINTS FOR ACTIVE CONTRACTIONS

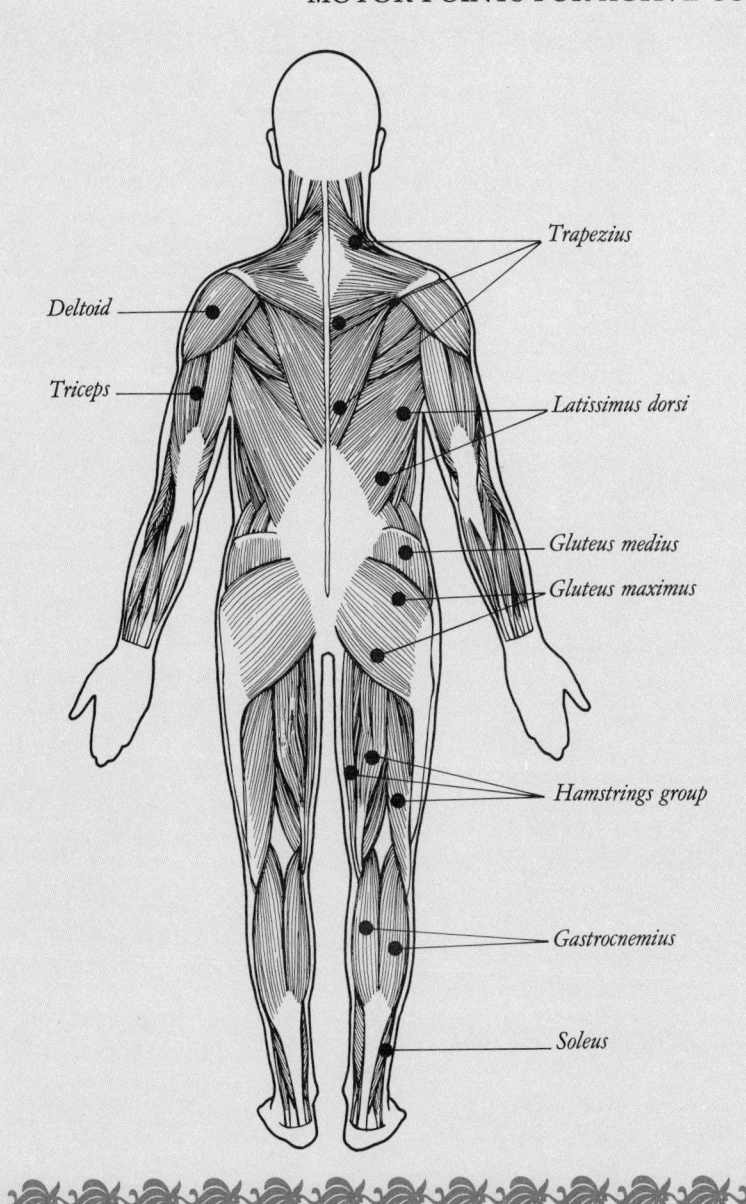

Deltoid

Triceps

Trapezius

Latissimus dorsi

Gluteus medius

Gluteus maximus

Hamstrings group

Gastrocnemius

Soleus

3

Suitability of treatment

CONTRA-INDICATIONS TO MUSCLE CONTRACTION

There are not many contra-indications to faradism because it is an action very similar to natural movement, but there are instances where it should not be applied or where medical guidance should be sought prior to treatment.

These contra-indications or instances where it would be unsuitable to apply faradism could be discovered at the initial figure consultation. If the client is unaware of her state of health, then it is advisable to ask her to check with her own doctor prior to treatment, especially as her figure plan may include many other factors (such as heat therapy, vacuum suction, etc.) which affect the circulatory, lymphatic and nervous systems.

Immediately before and during menstruation it is inadvisable and uncomfortable to treat the abdominal area. In pregnancy (especially during the early stages) it should not be applied, or after childbirth until medical permission is given. This is normally after the postnatal medical examination has been completed 6 weeks after the birth, but may be longer depending on the client's health and personal circumstances.

After operations, medical permission is again needed, and in the event of old scars in the treatment area, care should be taken to avoid discomfort if the skin has underlying adhesions or is taut and puckered. The abdominal area commonly has several scars, and operators must know the client's medical history before planning treatment.

A history of thrombosis (a blood clot in the vein) or phlebitis (inflammation of the veins) recorded on the client's record card would preclude treatment in the areas concerned. As a measure to prevent the formation of varicose veins the treatment is excellent, although when protruding veins are present, treatment should not be applied over them as they might become irritated and inflamed, forming varicose ulcers.

Any skin abrasions, open cuts, sunburn, etc., should be avoided as these will cause discomfort during the application, and could cause a tissue reaction, with the skin becoming raised, red and sore following treatment.

With a new client, it is wise to check the level of skin sensation in the area to be treated. If a client has a loss of sensation in the area, she would be unable to guide the therapist as to the comfortable levels of treatment, and the application could result in excessive muscle fatigue, soreness, etc. It might also point to a defect in the client's circulatory system such as swelling, oedema (fluid retention), etc., which would contra-indicate the treatment or require it to be adapted or another system used in preference (such as galvanic treatment for cellulite).

With older clients it is always a good idea to have them check their overall health with their doctor. Even if this is not a requirement stipulated by law (as it is in some countries) it is still excellent professional practice, and is the accepted procedure adopted by qualified therapists around the world. Then blood pressure, heart conditions, epilepsy, asthmatic problems, etc., are known about before the client starts treatment, which might well include other elements (such as saunas or steam baths) as well as faradism.

FIGURE DIAGNOSIS — INDICATIONS FOR MUSCLE TONING TREATMENT

Figure conditions which will benefit from muscle contraction will be evident to the experienced operator at the initial figure diagnosis. Simple figure assessment tests can be undertaken which show the state or tone of the muscles, their capacity to exercise, and will also guide the therapist as to the client's overall posture and mobility. A detailed figure diagnosis recorded on a clinic record card will provide essential measurements, weight, height, etc., and will determine the body type for weight guidance purposes. See *Body Treatments and Dietetics for the Beauty Therapist,* by Ann Gallant, for further detailed information on figure diagnosis and muscle testing procedures.

From this initial assessment the therapist will know how the client can be helped, and the extent of the figure problems to be overcome. Postural factors can be helped by exercise, weight problems by diet-linked programmes, and specific figure faults by clinic applications — including faradism.

In some cases muscle contraction will form the basis of the figure shaping, while in others it will combine with vacuum suction, vibratory massage or galvanic programmes for cellulite to get effective and fast results. Working out the ideal treatment

RECORD CARD

Body Treatment Card	Name		
Address		Tel. Work	
		Home	
Doctor	Medication	Smoke	Drink	Age
Medical history	Number of pregnancies	Ages of children	Recent post natal examination
Operations	Hysterectomy	Date	Caesarean section	Date
General health	Good	Poor	Constipation	High blood pressure	Varicose veins
Body condition	Overweight	Poor muscle tone	Underweight	Out of proportion
Treatment plan	General reduction	Specific reduction		
	Massage/relaxation	Cellulite		
Treatments booked		Products used and advised	
Treatments completed			

Date		Date	

Diet plan Name:

- Moderate protein/low carbohydrate
- Elimination diet
- Moderate protein/low fat/low carbohydrate
- Carbohydrate unit diet

			Date		
Weight					
Height					
Measurements					
1 Bust, chest					
2 Waist					
3 Hips					
4 Thigh left					
Thigh right					
5 Knee					
6 Calf					
7 Ankle					
8 Wrist					
9 Upper arm					

Figure and posture faults

Rounded shoulders	Spinal curvature
Abdominal weakness	Cellulite on thighs
Adipose deposits on buttocks	Weak inside thighs
	Fluid on knees
Tension in upper back	Heavy lower legs

Exercise plan

combination for the client's condition and specific figure problem is skilled figure diagnosis work. If the main effect and long term benefit of each system of treatment is known, then these effects can be combined for safe, fast results.

Muscle contraction works to reshape the body, toning and firming, changing the shape but not the weight of the body. Where a body weight problem is also present, then a diet must be introduced so that the client would then lose inches/cm and bulk or weight. She would then change shape and overall size.

GENERAL REDUCTION

Muscle contraction is most effective when used on clients within 6 to 9 kg (kilograms) (14 to 20 lb) approximately of their correct weight for their height and build, rather than on those who are severely overweight. This does not mean it cannot be used on really overweight people, but that its application is less effective, and it may prove quite difficult to gain a response from the muscles because of the blocking or buffer effect of the fatty tissue layer underlying the skin. Skin prickling may also prove unpleasant as the electrical activity is unable to trace a path to the muscles' motor points, because of their location deep under fatty layers. Other treatments such as heating routines (steam baths, saunas, etc.), natural exercise classes, and diet guidance will be more useful initially. Muscle contraction does have a part to play in re-establishing awareness of muscle tone on obese people, and can be used as an incentive on heavy clients to get them down to a size where passive muscle toning can really help them shape and firm their figures.

Where an overall weight loss is necessary, it has to be achieved through a reduced diet programme, well supported by regular clinic treatments to encourage the client's efforts and speed results. Regular treatments, including muscle contraction, will ensure that the weight disappears from the correct parts of the body, leaving it an attractive as well as a smaller shape. Without either regular exercise — which many clients seem loath to participate in — or regular salon sessions of muscle toning, clients who lose weight can sometimes end up looking very unattractive, with hanging floppy muscles, loose skin folds, and soft skin tone and texture. Both regular treatment with muscle contraction and massage with oils can avoid this problem occurring, so they should be actively promoted even to the extremely overweight individual embarking on a plan of reduction.

As weight is lost through diet, the effects of muscle toning will gradually be felt more clearly, and when eventually the muscles actually respond to the electrical charge and an active contraction is produced, the client will know she is really winning.

SPECIFIC REDUCTION

Clients who need to reduce and reshape simultaneously will benefit most from muscle contraction, and they are the ones who make up a large percentage of salon clients. So it is a popular service for them, and a profitable and effective one for the clinic. Figure shaping, or a reduction of inches/cm in one area of the body only, often termed *specific reduction,* is the most common and popular application of muscle contraction. It could more accurately be called figure shaping, as that is the main role it plays in the overall figure improvement, helping natural exercise to shape the body.

Muscle contraction has many uses. It can be given to help regain the figure after childbirth, for toning the pectoral muscles underlying the breasts, for shortening the rectus abdominis muscle, to flatten the abdominal area, and to re-establish a waistline by exercising the external and internal oblique muscles.

It can also be used to pull lazy muscles back into action, or given to firm and maintain a figure to avoid figure faults developing.

In all these instances muscle contraction acts in the same way as natural exercise, and is enhanced by the client following an exercise programme. For however well applied muscle contraction is, it is still passive exercise, and can never match the overall circulatory and respiratory benefits of active isotonic exercise. Once clients feel their muscles gaining in strength, their willingness to exercise naturally increases, so therapists should always encourage additional activity — in any form.

The special advantage of muscle toning, that of very specific or concentrated work on weak or unwilling, lazy muscles, needs the reinforcement of active movement, if muscle re-education and physical strength and tone in the body generally is ever to be achieved. Muscle contraction has an important role in the process, but it cannot replace natural effort.

RESHAPING AND FIRMING

Clients who are discontented with their appearance can be helped towards an improvement, using different systems of treatment (including muscle toning), once the *cause* of the problem is known.

If the condition is associated with adipose (fatty) deposits, circulatory defects, oedema (fluid retention–swelling), or a combination of these often referred to as *cellulite,* then a combined programme can be established. The emphasis on either muscle contraction or galvanic iontophoresis for cellulite will depend on whether the problem is caused more by weak muscles, so needing toning, or by fluid retention, needing galvanic iontophoresis. Both aspects of treatment form part of a cellulite routine, which combines peeling, pre-heating, massage, vacuum massage or muscle contraction, concluded by galvanism using specialized products for cellulite which have a diuretic action on the body (aiding fluid release). See *Beauty Guide 3, Galvanic Treatment* by Ann Gallant for further information.

Stubborn weight deposits have many systems of treatment, most based on increasing the general activity in the area, improving circulation and elimination aspects. This helps to make the established fatty subcutaneous deposits available to the body to be used up as food or energy sources when the client follows a reduction diet. This ensures that weight goes from the right areas of the body, those that offend the client or spoil her contours. Very hard established fat deposits require some pre-softening measures prior to muscle contraction, vacuum suction or vibratory applications, to make the treatment more comfortable and acceptable to the client. Steam baths, saunas, jacuzzis or heat lamps can all be used, and this pre-heating really adds to the effectiveness of the application, improving quite dramatically the results obtained. This is especially so with electrical systems such as faradism and galvanism, where with good skin preparation much lower levels of electrical current can be used to produce effective results, improving client acceptance considerably.

Reshaping the actual contours of the body can be very effectively achieved with faradism, including lifting and shaping of the breast muscles, slimming the lines of the thighs, tightening and firming the buttocks, and flattening and holding in the waistline.

Muscle contraction can also be used as a back up to figure building with small hand-held weights to increase the muscles underlying the breasts themselves. As muscles only develop slowly against an increasing load or weight, muscle contraction cannot really build muscle, only tone it and increase its strength and improve its shape. If the client is using small hand-held weights and exercising regularly, increasing the weights' use progressively, then muscles will slowly build and new muscle fibres develop. This can be seen more clearly in male body-builders, who are able to develop muscles very specifically and increase their bulk. Apart from breast muscles, women seldom need to build muscles to obtain an attractive shape, and so only need toning and tightening aspects, which muscle contraction can easily provide.

This is an important point to understand and discuss with clients, as some women worry about building muscles they do not want and becoming masculine in appearance. The essential principle that muscle contraction of any type cannot build muscle — unless against an increasing load or resistance — can be explained to dispel anxiety. Of course, muscles in their normal role in life will, over an extended period, eventually show an increase in size. This is seen when people are involved in physical work or sports activities, but it occurs over a very long period. Anybody who has undertaken an intensive training in ballet, or participated in horse riding or swimming, etc., at a formative time in their muscle development (age 9 to 14), will know how muscles can develop from constant and repetitive actions.

This is one reason why it is important to test muscle strength rather carefully on the initial diagnosis, using special exercises against resistance. (See *Body Treatments and Dietetics for the Beauty Therapist* by Ann Gallant for reference.) For it may be that the client has not got a problem of weak muscles, but that the problem relates more to subcutaneous fatty deposits, fluid retention, poor circulation, etc. Very seldom will anti-gravity muscles like the thighs really need toning as they are in a state of conscious tone or contraction at all times while awake, to help keep the skeleton upright and make movements possible. Rather, it is the muscles that only assist or help in these anti-gravity actions that suffer more from lack of tone — such as the inside thighs, round the waistline, abdominal areas, underlying the breasts, and the inside upper arm.

APPLICATIONS FOR MUSCLE CONTRACTION — WHEN TO USE TO ADVANTAGE

SPECIFIC REDUCTION AND RESHAPING
(1) Postnatal — after postnatal medical examination, 6 to 8 weeks after the birth.
(2) Disuse of abdominal muscles — poor postural stance.
(3) Following weight loss or immobility.
(4) Reshaping of thighs and buttocks out of proportion to the rest of body.
(5) Lifting and firming the bust area, by working the underlying muscles.
(6) Upper arm toning (may be included in a breast toning layout).
(7) Inside thigh toning and tightening.
(8) Reshaping of thighs and lower legs if necessary to improve overall contours.

GENERAL REDUCTION AND STRENGTHENING PROGRAMME
(1) Overall toning in association with reduction diet programme and in association with other treatments. Toning of the breasts, upper arms, abdominal area, buttocks, thighs, and lower legs if necessary.
(2) Reshaping and strengthening of the waistline to reduce a paunch in men.

(3) Strengthening of weak abdominal muscles after multiple pregnancies or after hysterectomy or caesarean operation (medical approval required and medical liaison essential).

MAINTENANCE PLANS

(1) Waistline maintenance in men to prevent thickening of the waistline.
(2) Maintenance of a good figure to keep it in peak form.
(3) Maintaining the figure improvement results obtained following a reduction and reshaping programme.

4

Practical points

ENSURING EFFECTIVE CONTRACTIONS

MOTOR POINTS

It has been seen that all superficial muscles can be exercised or stimulated most effectively on their motor points. If the location of these motor points is known, then regardless of which type of pad layout is used, good clear comfortable contractions will result when the pads are accurately placed and an adequate amount of current applied. When pad placing is inaccurate the current is unable to make good contact and is ineffective, also the client suffers discomfort.

The therapist should know the attachments and positions of the main muscles of the body which make up the bulk and shape of the figure. Then, even if the client is overweight, the muscles' bone attachments can be used for guidance for accurate pad placing.

SUBCUTANEOUS FAT

Several factors conspire to prevent clear motor point stimulation. Excessive subcutaneous fat overlying the muscles in an area acts as a barrier to the current, so accuracy of pad placing is vital on the more overweight clients. Reinforced padding layouts may also need to be used to help achieve muscle activity without undue client discomfort in the area. Meticulous attention to skin preparation and pre-heating the area is also needed.

SKIN PREPARATION

Poor skin preparation, in addition to the natural resistance of the skin to the electrode, is another factor to consider. The latest pads are much improved in their capacity to allow a good passage or flow of electrical current to pass through them to activate the muscle's motor point. They only require moistening on their working surface before being applied to the skin, and strapped firmly to maintain skin contact.

However, if the pad or the skin is not clean, or has a film of natural body oil or massage oil still present on it, contractions will be very poor or impossible and in all instances the client will feel excessive prickling and discomfort in the skin under the pad because oil is a very effective barrier to electrical current. If the client uses an oil-based body lotion, or regularly uses sun-tan oil, this can be present in the skin's layers although it may not be apparent on its surface. Washing the skin quickly with warm soapy water or a body wash product is a good substitute for pre-heating measures (steam baths, saunas, etc.) if time is limited. This washing breaks down skin resistance, removes residual oil — natural or not — and leaves the skin moist, clean and warm.

SKIN TEMPERATURE

Any warmth produced in the skin reduces the level of current intensity required to obtain an effective contraction, and so improves client comfort. The pre-warming cuts down the initial skin sensation experienced — prickling under the pads — and brings the muscles more quickly over this stage into active visible contractions, which feel natural and comfortable to the body. This prickling under the pads is termed the *primary reaction* and is caused by sensory nerve reactions in the skin under the pads. It occurs until sufficient power or amount of current is present in the right place — the active motor point area of the muscle — to bring about muscle stimulation and contraction. This primary reaction can be unnerving for the client, so all measures that act to get the contractions quickly to an active level should be used.

So motor point accuracy, careful skin preparation, warmth in the tissues, clean pads and skilful application of the faradic system, all play a part in giving effective and comfortable muscle toning treatments.

5

Principles of faradic padding

BASIC PADDING LAYOUTS

Once the initial figure assessment and tests for muscle strength have been completed to determine the client's figure needs, a padding layout for muscle contraction can be devised to improve the figure problem.

Normally padding is used which divides the body into left and right sides, and this is termed a *split body* padding. This allows differences in the two sides of the body to be balanced by separately controlling the intensity of the current used. With this method, differences in muscle bulk, tone of muscles, etc., on either side of the body can be balanced to obtain equal movements in the overall application. The group activity of the muscles is also noted, and if an area would work naturally using all the muscles in a co-ordinated manner, then this is how they are padded. For instance, one thigh would be padded completely using several sets of pads to create a natural contraction movement. Then the second thigh would be padded using several more sets of pads in a similar manner. The positions of the pads on each thigh might be identical, but they are padded separately and controlled on the machine's individual outlets separately. Then if through natural development (right or left handedness), sports development, or old injuries (fractures, etc.), one side of the body appears stronger or weaker than the other, this difference can be balanced by using different levels of current intensity on each side of the body.

SPECIFIC PADDING

The individual pairs of pads may be placed along the length of the muscles, this being one of the clearest methods of muscle contraction, working the muscle along its long axis. Each muscle in an area such as the front thigh (quadriceps), would therefore have a pair of pads on each superficial section. So the rectus femoris (front most anterior thigh), the vastus medialis (front inside thigh, closest to the midline of the body) and the vastus lateralis (outside thigh, furthest away from the midline of the body), would all have a pair of pads placed on them. The fourth section of the quadriceps lies under the rectus femoris and cannot be stimulated directly; however, it works when the rest of the group moves the thigh.

A SPLIT BODY PADDING

A group padding layout for generally toning the abdomen/waist, and thigh areas (if required)

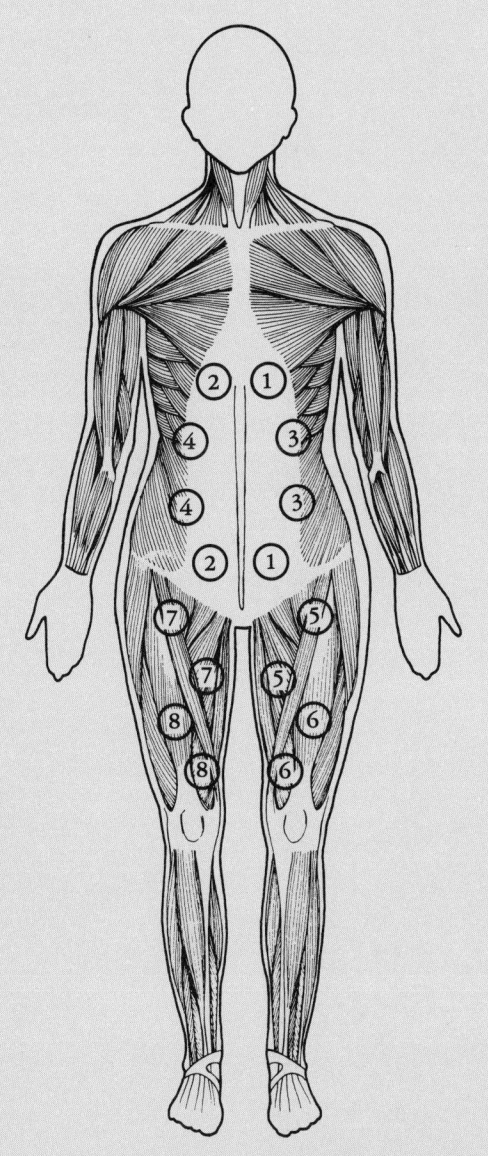

MASTER PLANS FOR PADDING LAYOUTS

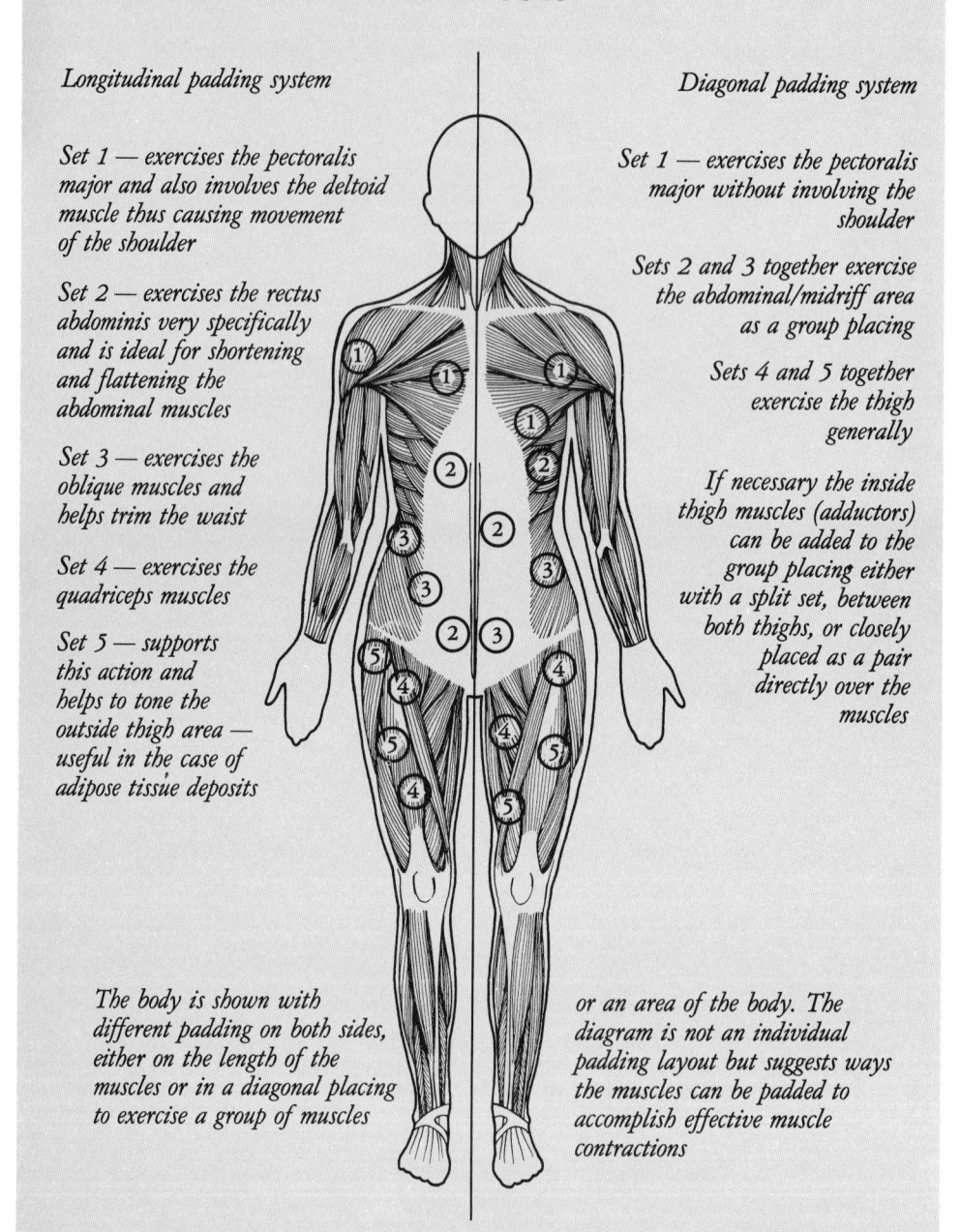

Longitudinal padding system

Set 1 — exercises the pectoralis major and also involves the deltoid muscle thus causing movement of the shoulder

Set 2 — exercises the rectus abdominis very specifically and is ideal for shortening and flattening the abdominal muscles

Set 3 — exercises the oblique muscles and helps trim the waist

Set 4 — exercises the quadriceps muscles

Set 5 — supports this action and helps to tone the outside thigh area — useful in the case of adipose tissue deposits

Diagonal padding system

Set 1 — exercises the pectoralis major without involving the shoulder

Sets 2 and 3 together exercise the abdominal/midriff area as a group placing

Sets 4 and 5 together exercise the thigh generally

If necessary the inside thigh muscles (adductors) can be added to the group placing either with a split set, between both thighs, or closely placed as a pair directly over the muscles

The body is shown with different padding on both sides, either on the length of the muscles or in a diagonal placing to exercise a group of muscles or an area of the body. The diagram is not an individual padding layout but suggests ways the muscles can be padded to accomplish effective muscle contractions

Muscles that are natural antagonists must NOT be exercised simultaneously

26

Working muscles in this way causes the greatest degree of muscle shortening, and allows the muscles to contract as fully as possible. It is normally referred to as a *longitudinal* placing of pads — simply meaning along the length of the muscle.

GENERAL PADDING

Apart from these very specific placings, the area can also be exercised in a more general way — still with the body divided into two sides, but with the pads applied in a more general manner in the treatment area. Then the action created will come from the overall reaction of all the pads applied and interacting in the area. The pads cause a general level of activity which creates muscle action on all the muscle tissue lying under the total area of the pads. This system is not so accurate but can be used where more general toning is needed, or where maintenance effects are required rather than specific shortening or tightening. It can be used as an alternative padding technique for the thighs/buttocks area, and is applied by placing the pads diagonally in pairs, until the whole area to be treated is complete. It may employ a similar number of pads to the longitudinal method, or even more in a reinforced padding layout on a heavier client, but they are not paired along the individual muscles' length.

If pads are not placed in close proximity to the motor points of the muscles in an area, much of the current is ineffective — so even with these more general paddings, attention to the motor point positions is essential. The current will attempt to reach the active area of the muscles, and in the process can cause discomfort and distress to the client. Even with a general padding, if all motor points of the muscles are covered, the whole area will be suffused with faradic-type current and when sufficient current is applied, active contractions will occur.

TRANSFERENCE OF CURRENT

When pads are placed in an area to be exercised, a transfer of current seems to occur, with some of the current not going directly to the motor point of the muscles. Some seeps away and is ineffective, and some affects connecting or associated muscles in the area. This alters the current intensity needed on muscles to be exercised in the surrounding areas, when pads are subsequently placed to reinforce the effect of the overall contraction.

On some areas of the body this is more evident than others, and the effect can be clearly seen in an area of rather weak muscles such as the abdominal muscles, which are not prime movers in their own right but work to support body movements, rather than instigate or start them. When the length of the rectus abdominis is padded from the sternum to the pubis area and the muscle is working actively, pads placed on the oblique muscles either side of the body will be found to need very little intensity to gain active contractions, unless excessively weak. This is because of the current transference occurring from the rectus abdominis muscle itself. This transference occurs most in areas where the muscles are interlinked both anatomically and in their action, such as the abdominal area, where all muscles work together like a supporting corset not only to hold in the abdominal contents, but to act together in steadying many other body movements, such as lifting and rotation.

DECIDING THE ACTION NEEDED

When deciding how to pad an area, *it is important to think of the effect really needed.* If shortening of an overstretched muscle is needed, such as the rectus abdominis after pregnancy, then longitudinal padding is the clearest and best way to achieve the effect, and the muscle may need to be worked in isolation for a few treatments to avoid it being supported in its action by the stronger muscles such as the oblique muscles. These supporting muscles may then be added to the padding layout as the rectus abdominis becomes shorter between its two bone attachment points — sternum and pubic bones.

If, however, the abdominal area is simply weak and the client unable to hold in and flatten her abdomen because of poor posture, lazy habits, or poor tone caused by multiple pregnancies, operations, etc., then general toning and strengthening will be more effective and provide results more quickly. Then the whole area can be padded, and the muscles' action balanced so they are contracting in a similar way to a natural abdominal retraction — being held in and working deeply into the body, like an isometric exercise. This very quickly retrains the muscles, and makes the client very aware of the potential strength of her muscles, and it encourages her home efforts. This shows the importance of knowing the individual strength of the muscles through testing during the initial figure assessment.

As the abdominal muscles can be exercised locally — that is, not affecting the rest of the body — a very concentrated effect can be created with muscle contraction on this problem area, bringing excellent results. By working this way, the other stronger areas of the body cannot *carry* the weak abdominal muscles, as does occur when natural exercise routines are given, unless they are cleverly worked out specifically to avoid this happening. The strong muscles of the thighs can, in an exercise such as sitting up from a lying down position, simply pull the trunk up into the sitting position by their strength alone, and the abdominal muscles are simply carried in the action. They need not work at all, and this is why the abdominal area is such a problem area.

The weak muscles can be isolated in natural exercise routines, by removing the stronger muscles' capacity to work so effectively; for example, by lifting the feet from the ground, bending the knees, etc., but this can be difficult and muscle contraction has therefore a very valuable role to play in the rehabilitation of the waistline through exercise.

Some areas of the body can be treated together with the ten outlet faradic system, and as long as the muscles padded are not antagonistic in their action towards each other, this is acceptable and time saving. If an area has difficulty in contracting well, owing to weakness, fat deposits, sensitivity, etc., it is better initially for it to be exercised on its own, and only later for it to be added into a multi-area padding treatment. It can be rather nerve wracking for the client to be over-padded, and overall it is not often the most effective way to get results. Keeping the client's trust and seeing she is at ease with the treatment is also important.

MATCHING NATURAL MOVEMENTS

If in doubt about the comfort of padding several areas and exercising them together, it is sensible to see if the body could achieve the movement naturally. For example, contraction of the pectoral muscles, the rectus abdominis, and the internal/external oblique muscles together is a fairly natural action, and with training the client could achieve the activity naturally. But adding in the front aspect of the thighs as well to the overall padding could prove fatiguing, and it could be better to work the trunk on its own, followed by the thighs, or thighs and buttocks together (either within the same treatment or later in the week). It all depends on the client's general condition and muscular tone.

In the same way, the buttocks, back thighs and front thighs could all be padded at once on a reasonably fit person, within 6 to 7 kg (14 lb) of ideal body weight, without causing any discomfort, as long as actual opposing muscles (antagonists) are not involved. If the client can naturally perform this type of overall contraction, isometrically, then it can be reproduced artificially by muscle contraction. It is often a matter of getting the client to concentrate on the action needed, and then she can perform it correctly. This is real muscle re-education in action, and can be achieved by both natural and muscle toning means.

On a rather overweight individual it would be more effective to divide the routine into abdominal and front thighs, and buttocks and back thighs areas, giving each area a good chance to work comfortably and really getting clear visible levels of contraction. It may be that the same length of treatment time is given, but the application is divided between the two areas, so that each can work to its greatest potential, so improving the muscle tone.

GENERAL PADDING LAYOUT

Padding for the abdomen, hips and thighs where the client is out of proportion and needs reshaping. The back and front of the body may be padded simultaneously if this does not appear uncomfortable to the client, or cause excessive body movement

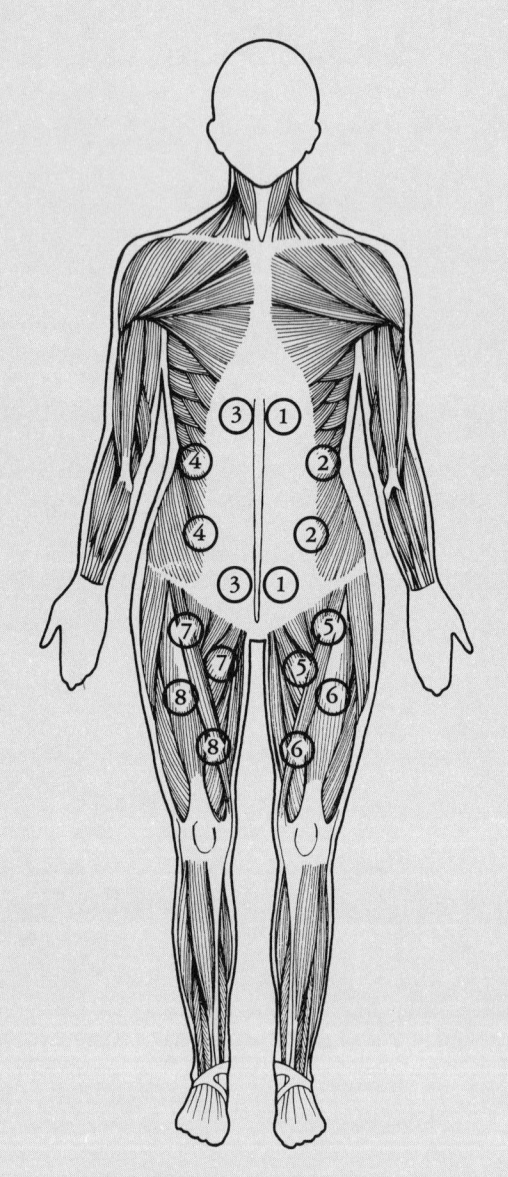

This is a general padding, based on longitudinal and diagonal padding. The body is split, divided into right and left sides

BUTTOCKS

The need to work each area very clearly and specifically, working for clear visible contractions to avoid discomfort, is especially true of applications on the buttocks' area; an area being naturally well covered with subcutaneous fat acts as a very effective barrier to faradic-type current, which has a job to reach the active motor point area of the muscles. Reinforced padding is often needed to obtain sufficient power in the area to bring about a contraction. More pads are applied to support the action, and the upper part of the hamstring muscle group of the back of the thigh is also exercised to help the buttocks and thighs to work well, that is, as they would in a natural buttocks' contraction.

As the motor point areas for the buttocks are so well hidden, a more general padding on the buttocks themselves is normal, still relating to the positions of the muscles which will bring about the contraction. Activating the motor point of the major muscles of the area — gluteus maximus/minimus — the sciatic nerve can also be rather painful, and paddings are therefore placed to obtain good contractions close to, but not directly over, the sciatic nerve position. It is more a question of putting enough muscular activity/current intensity into the area, working at the skin preparation, heat, warmth, moisture, cleanliness aspects, and ensuring pads are well placed and that there are enough of them, and that they are well strapped. Working more at the different factors that can prevent a good contraction on this difficult area.

NERVES OF THE RIGHT LEG — POSTERIOR (BACK) VIEW

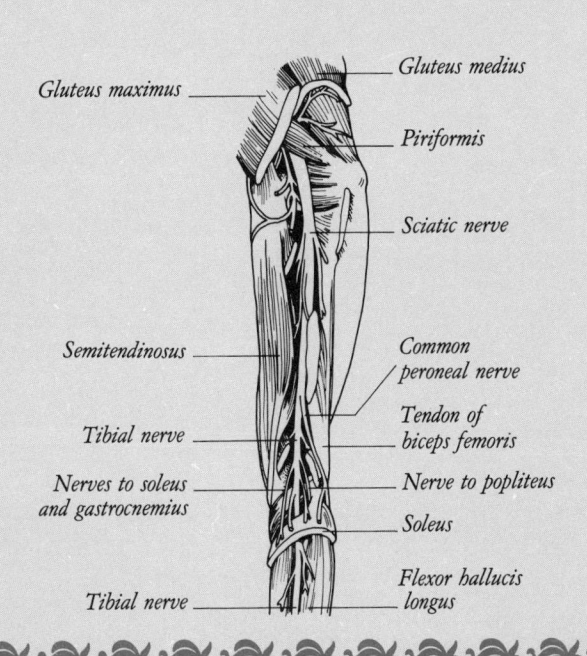

PADDING FOR THE BUTTOCKS IN A LINKED ABDOMEN/HIPS AND THIGHS PLACEMENT

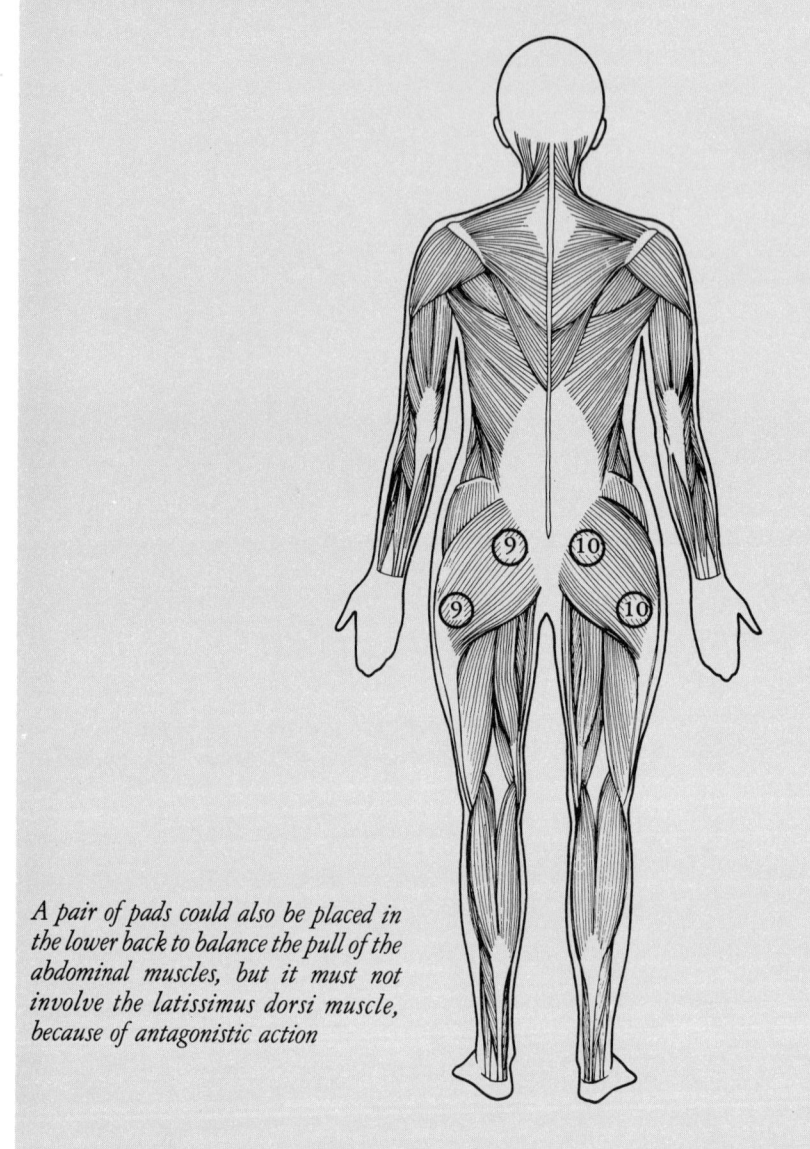

A pair of pads could also be placed in the lower back to balance the pull of the abdominal muscles, but it must not involve the latissimus dorsi muscle, because of antagonistic action

A REINFORCED BUTTOCKS LAYOUT

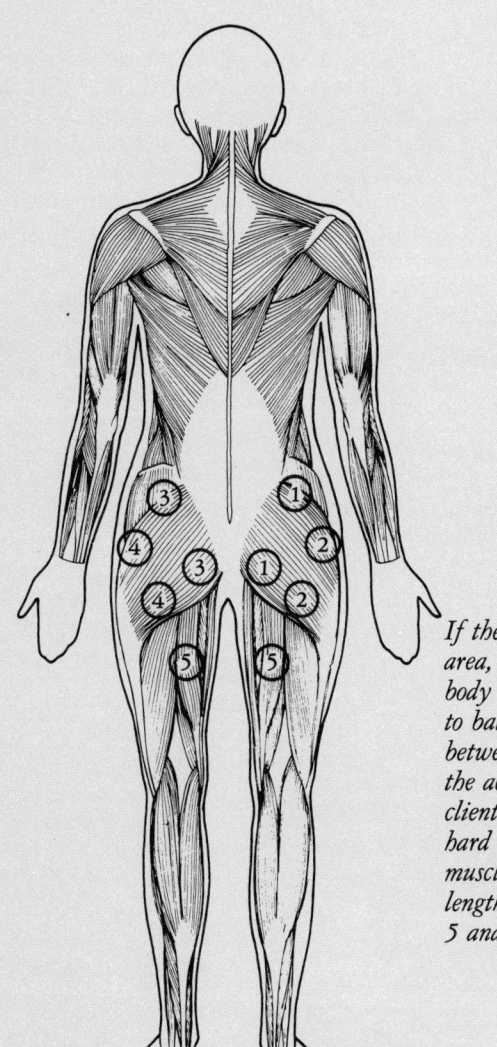

If the client is really overweight in the area, pads 1–2–3–4 are placed on a split body method (each side separately controlled to balance contractions). Pads 5 are shared between both sides of the body to support the action of the gluteal padding. If the client is really overweight, and contractions hard to achieve, the pads on the hamstring muscles may be placed in pairs along the length of the muscles — giving sets 5 and 6.

BREASTS

Breasts can be improved in their position on the chest wall, and by activating the whole underlying pectoralis major/minor muscle areas, the skin of the breasts also receives additional stimulation which helps support cosmetic treatment programmes designed to firm and tighten the skin.

The split body padding system is normally used if specific toning of the underlying breast tissue is needed, such as post-pregnancy work. This is an ideal method as the breasts often show marked differences either side of the body. The pads are placed above and below the breasts, a pair on the right and a pair on the left side. The lower pads are tucked tightly up close to the breasts, otherwise through transference of current and interconnection, the rectus abdominis muscle will become involved in the movement. This is not harmful, but it prevents the desired concentration of effect on the pectoralis muscles, and can sometimes cause cramp in the rectus abdominis muscle.

This split body method is preferable for all toning, lifting and postnatal work, as it enables equal contractions to be made on both sides of the body, by adjusting the intensity of the individual controls to balance the action.

When a client is simply maintaining her figure and is slim, a pair of pads split between the two sides of the body will be adequate to exercise the breast muscles. When the client is having a general toning treatment applied to the abdominal area, and perhaps the thighs, and is quite happy and adjusted to the routine, any extra pads remaining free in the faradic system can be slipped into the bra straps to tone this area. This helps the client to feel she is getting her money's worth. It all depends how the client is coping with the application.

When treating the breast area, pads should be positioned so that most of the action will be contained within the bulk of the pectoralis major area, and not involve its connection into the upper arm bone — the humerus. If the humerus is involved, it causes the shoulder to pull forwards, which feels awkward. If this occurs unduly, the upper pads can be moved slightly inwards and downwards away from the tendon area of the pectoralis muscles where they attach into the bone of the upper arm.

ARMS

The inside upper arm is a difficult area to exercise naturally, but can be very effectively treated by artificial muscle toning. A natural isometric-type contraction should be obtained, which does not affect the shoulder or elbow joints unduly. If the upper back and shoulders are rounded, with poor postural stance, then this can be

BREAST AND ARM PADDING SUGGESTIONS

Maintenance — one pair of pads shared by pectoral muscles

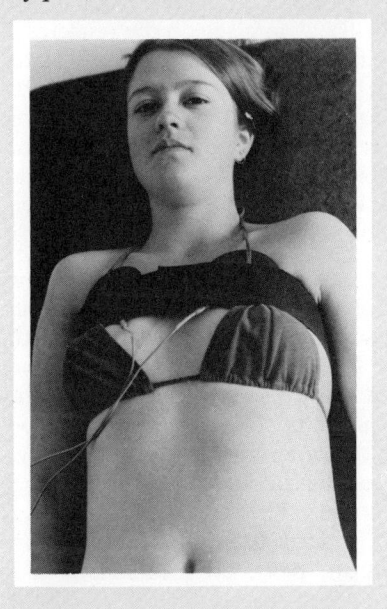

Toning and firming — breasts and upper arms

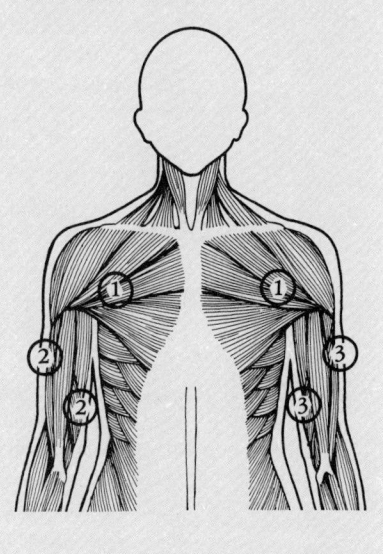

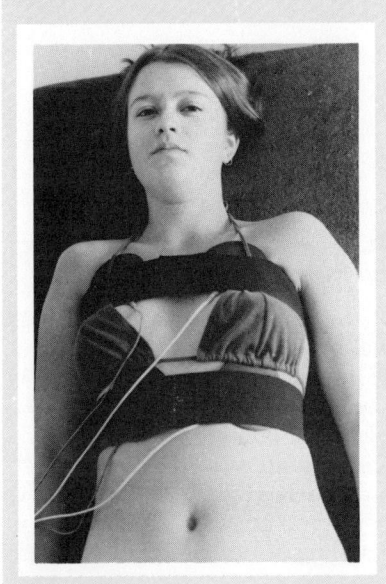

Post-pregnancy improvement

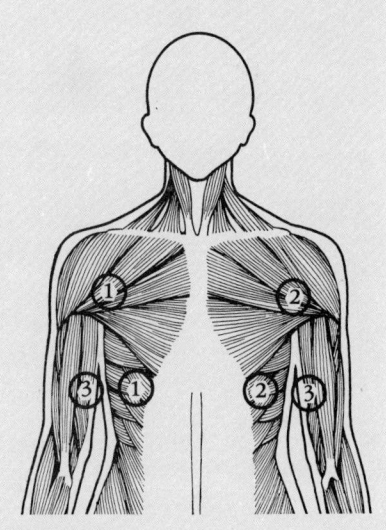

Maintenance in the older woman — breasts and upper arms

35

padded at the same time, which will pull the shoulders backwards, straightening the back and tightening the inside arm. The level of contraction need not be very active to be effective, and should not cause the shoulders to hunch upwards. Pads can be placed on the trapezius muscle, both sides from one outlet, and each arm padded separately. The upper back pads will stay in place on the muscles if the client is lying comfortably on the couch with her body weight holding them in place. The arm pads can be strapped firmly, with two pads in place on each arm, along the length of the muscle, or either side of the arm, as long as the triceps and biceps are not padded in opposition to each other. This would be an antagonistic action, causing the arm to attempt to push and pull simultaneously, which would be unnatural and confusing.

The arms and shoulders can be treated together, again at a low level of contraction, tensing and relaxing in the same manner as an isometric action. The deltoid muscle can be exercised, again with one outlet split between the two sides of the body to reduce the effect on this strong muscle. This will cause the shoulders to lift, and when the arms are also brought up to an active level, the contraction will cause the arms to tighten into the side of the body. Watching the action created will tell the therapist if she has the pad placings correct. Once more this copies a very natural body action, but one that in normal life is seldom used, hence common problems with upper back tension, pain, etc., and slack unattractive arms.

GENERAL POINTS FOR EFFECTIVE CONTRACTIONS

To judge whether a pad placing is likely to work well, certain points need looking at.

(1) If pads are not placed accurately over motor points, contractions will not be comfortable, and may even be unobtainable.

(2) If the load or resistance that the muscle contraction has to carry is excessive, contractions will be difficult to obtain and the muscle stimulation will need to be helped to achieve a contraction by reinforcing the effect with more pads. This is termed *reinforced padding*. The habit of placing a pair of outlets — one pad on each thigh on the rectus femoris muscle — is an example of incorrect padding. The task the muscle stimulation has to achieve is excessive for it, and it causes spasmodic or uneven contractions. A pair of pads on each thigh (split body padding — longitudinal placing) produces a better result.

(3) The placing must never make muscles work against each other. As natural antagonists, the back and the front of the body

should not be worked together, as it cannot lean forward and bend backwards at the same time, and should not be asked to do so artificially. Anything which does not produce a natural movement will not be helping the body back to natural strength and tone in its muscles.

(4) Sufficient pads must be used to permit clear contractions. A slim well-toned person will produce contractions with very few pads and low levels of intensity, as she will offer very little resistance to muscular stimulation. A larger person presents more resistance, a larger load, a bigger task, and padding must reflect this with clear paddings — long axis placings as much as possible, reinforced paddings where necessary, and real attention to accuracy of motor points. Skin preparation, pre-heating aspects, etc., all need extra care, for the larger person has to be helped more if she is to achieve good contractions without discomfort.

(5) The job the muscle contraction has to do must be reflected in the padding, and the manner in which the treatment is applied. A decision must be made whether to tone or maintain an area, reduce the length of a muscle, strengthen an entire area, tighten and tone the muscles and skin overall while a weight loss is in progress, pull in an ageing paunch, lift and tone the breast supporting muscles or firm flabby contours present through illness or lack of exercise. Paddings can then be devised to work muscles specifically along their length, or exercise them in groups, or cover a whole area, or combine both methods to achieve overall toning effects, and in some cases use reinforced paddings where extra help and muscle stimulation are needed.

(6) The way muscles work naturally should be closely followed in the padding layouts. For example it would be very unnatural for the buttocks to contract one side at a time, so they should always be artificially stimulated so that both sides work evenly at the same time. Likewise the trapezius muscle of the upper back works evenly along both sides of its spine attachments for most movements, and this is how it should be exercised. The thigh muscles work in groups — quadriceps at the front and hamstrings at the back, and these are the actions that should be copied, not parts of the group worked separately, piece by piece, as they could not work this way in nature.

PADDING LAYOUT TO HELP CORRECT PROTRUSION OF THE ABDOMINAL WALL

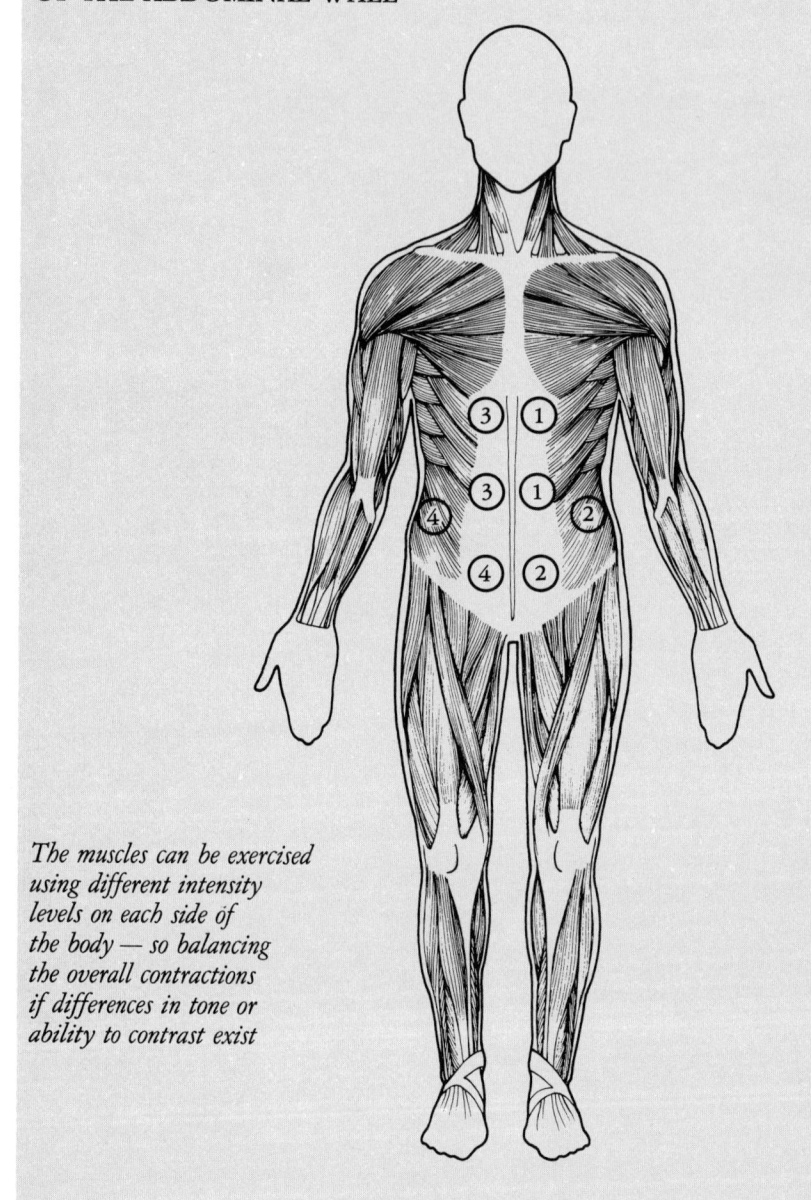

The muscles can be exercised using different intensity levels on each side of the body — so balancing the overall contractions if differences in tone or ability to contrast exist

PADDING FOR MIDRIFF AND TRUNK

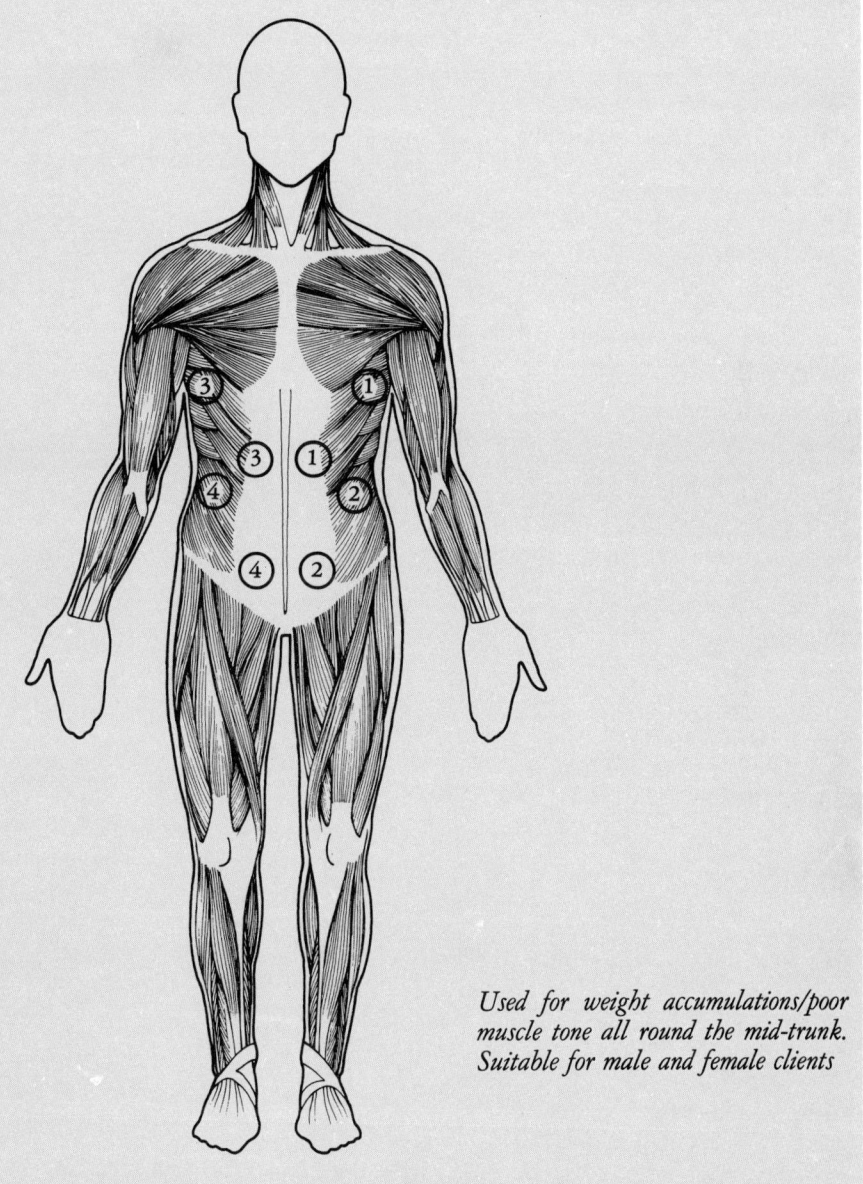

Used for weight accumulations/poor muscle tone all round the mid-trunk. Suitable for male and female clients

39

PADDING LAYOUTS FOR THE BACK OF THE BODY

Set 1 — shows a placing which is used to relieve tension in the trapezius muscle

Set 2 — shows a placing used as a reinforcement to prevent backache when there is a concentration of pads on the abdomen

Both sets 1 and 2 are termed split sets; that is the pads are split or divided between both sides of the body

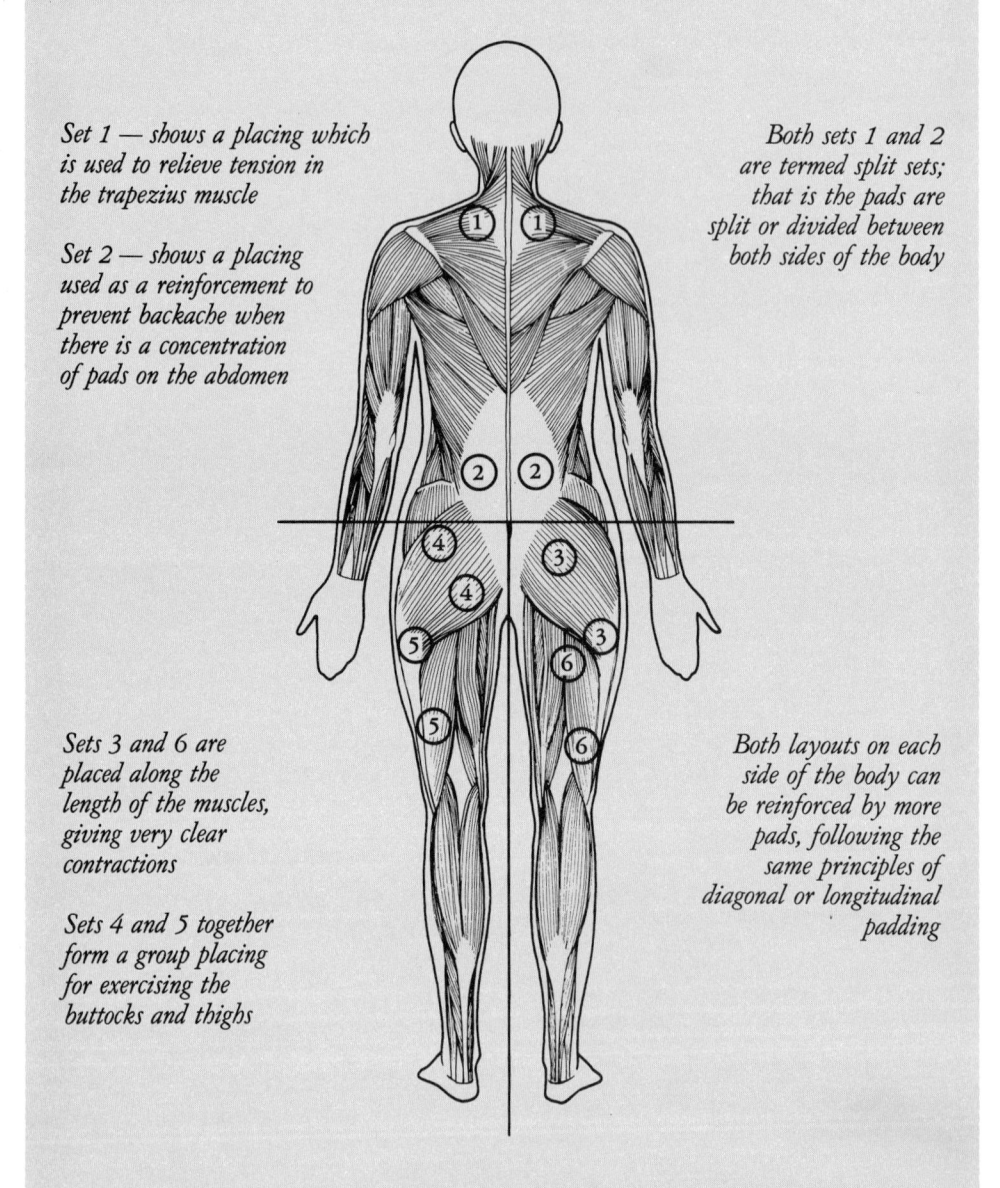

Sets 3 and 6 are placed along the length of the muscles, giving very clear contractions

Sets 4 and 5 together form a group placing for exercising the buttocks and thighs

Both layouts on each side of the body can be reinforced by more pads, following the same principles of diagonal or longitudinal padding

GENERAL PADDING LAYOUT FOR THE BACK/BUTTOCKS

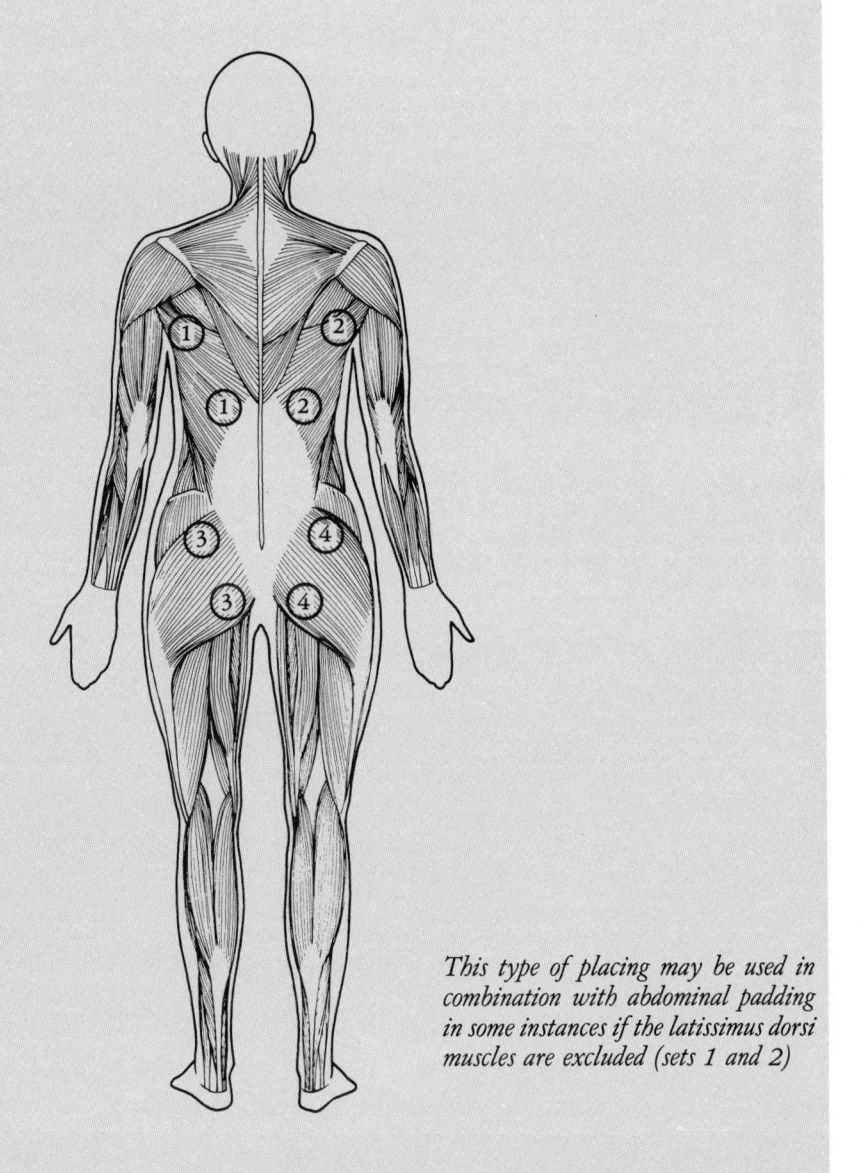

This type of placing may be used in combination with abdominal padding in some instances if the latissimus dorsi muscles are excluded (sets 1 and 2)

6

Applying muscle toning treatment

ORGANIZING THE TREATMENT

After the initial measurements of the figure have been taken, the decision about padding can be made to provide an effective sequence likely to bring good results. The largest measurement for each area can be recorded, very accurately if specific reduction is needed, more generally if overall reduction forms the basis of the treatment plan.

If the client is hoping to achieve a change in the shape of an area, then this should be discussed frankly, using a wall mirror if necessary to ensure the client understands what the problem is and how it can be solved, with her help as well as clinic treatments. Many minor changes possible with muscle toning cannot actually be recorded as a change in measurements, but the client will know an improvement is happening as her clothes get less tight and she begins to feel firmer. Toning of the buttocks is one example where measurements may stay constant on a reasonably slim person, but the contours will alter as the seat 'lifts' into a more firm taut shape.

The faradic system should be prepared and checked swiftly for firm contacts on the leads, outlets and pads. The pads should be placed ready for use in a storage tray as this avoids confusion and saves time on this closely booked treatment. With the *Beauty Gallery* the controls of the faradic system must all be at zero otherwise the unit will not function, this being a built-in safety feature.

The unit is switched on and its pulse set. It is generally used at the 'normal' setting, depending on the purpose of the application. If the ready light is on, the system is ready for use; if not, it indicates a knob is in the active position which must be rectified. The machine will then require switching off and on again, to get it into action. The therapist soon gets used to leaving her machine in the correct safe condition, where no shock, however small, can surprise the client when the treatment is starting.

The client can then be helped on to the prepared couch or chair, which has straps placed across it in readiness, to save time. Both chairs and couches can be used for muscle toning; as long as the client can rest comfortably she does not need to be flat on a bed, and some clients like to read which diverts their attention from the contractions. The back should be well supported and if it appears under strain, a small pillow support can be placed in the small of the back. The client should be made as comfortable as possible so that she can relax into the treatment.

The straps are then placed around the body areas and the pads slipped in underneath them in pairs to work the motor points, according to the padding plans suggested previously. The pads should be applied systematically, working from one end of the machine to the other, as this helps keep track of the muscles being exercised. Colour coding also helps in tracking the muscles being worked.

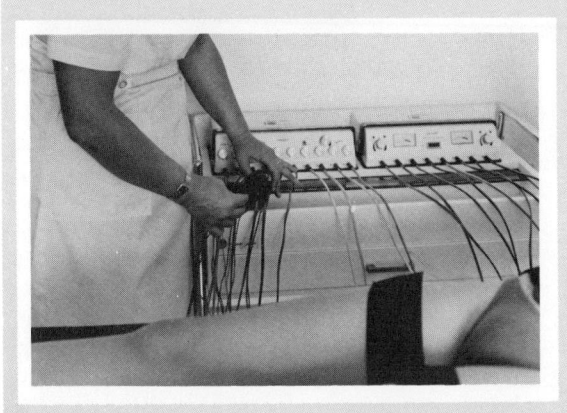

APPLYING THE PADS SYSTEMATICALLY

(a) Working to a method while padding and strapping speeds the application, and saves confusion

For example it is useful to use the first three pairs of outlets/pads on one thigh, the next three on the other thigh, and the last four on the abdominal or abdominal and breast areas. Then each part of the body is separately spaced on the machine, and can be controlled accurately, aided by the colour coding, with each outlet having a different colour completely on its lead.

FAST AND ACCURATE PADDING

Padding can be completed in many ways for speed and efficiency, but the operator needs a system which is not only fast but ensures client comfort and prevents errors occurring. It is helpful if a muscle or a group of muscles can be padded in sequence, and a double muscle like the rectus abdominis, which is separated by a tendinous band down the centre area, is padded on two adjacent outlets, and these two outlets can then be treated as one. This means the muscles are then exercised equally, both sides working simultaneously, and the movement does not then pull unnaturally to one side or the other. Likewise, the group action muscles such as the quadriceps, can be padded as a group with three outlets (6 pads — 2 on each superficial section of the large muscle), and these three outlets then increased simultaneously. Then the action is clear, and natural, and the thigh contracts steadily. Two legs can be treated together — six outlets (12 pads) — and minor differences in intensity needed can be adjusted as the intensity levels are increased, until the actual muscle action is equal and comfortable on both thighs.

(b) Three pairs of pads could be used on each thigh, leaving four pairs available for the abdominal area, or any other area needing treatment

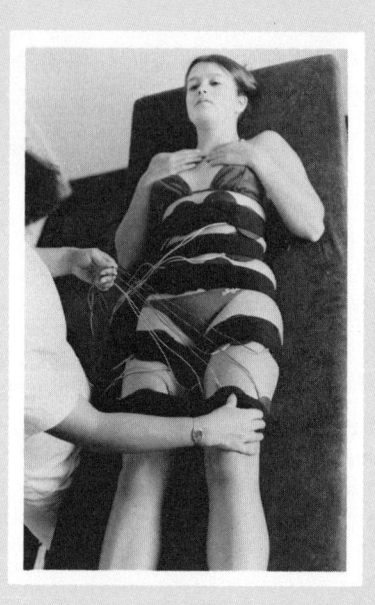

PLACING FOR COMFORT

Once the padding is complete, either by placing the pads into the prepared strapping, or applying them at the same time, pads and straps together, then the whole padding is checked for comfort and accuracy. Midline positions can be checked, that is the pads in relation to the midline of the body, and in relation to the muscles' bone attachment points, i.e. sternum, pelvic girdle, pubis, etc. The thighs should be checked for pad positions in relation to the knee joint and the actual positions of the muscles and their motor points. If in doubt, the client can be asked to form an active contraction naturally, and this tension in the muscle can be used to guide the placing of the pad, covering the motor point accurately.

Bones can always be used as guides for placing pads, the lower ribs and inside the iliac crest of the pelvic girdle for the oblique muscles, the lower sternum and pubis for the rectus abdominis, and the sternum and humerus for the pectoralis muscles. On most occasions, it is advisable to arrange the placing just a little away from the bone attachment to make the contraction comfortable as well as accurate. On some muscles it has been noticed that the motor point is just beyond the tendon area of the muscle, where it flares out to form the bulk of the muscle itself.

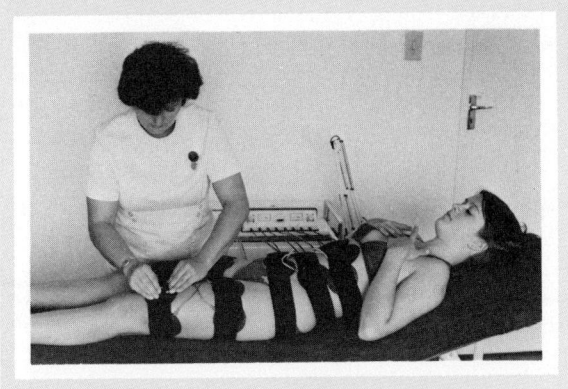

(c) Swiftly check all the pads for accuracy, contact and comfort, when the padding is complete

OBTAINING ACTIVE CONTRACTIONS

The client can quickly be put at ease about the treatment and the sensation explained to her. Treatment proceeds with the pulse at 'normal' and the ready light on. The intensity of the current is steadily and gradually increased until the prickling stage passes and visible contractions are evident. The intensity may be increased a muscle at a time, or more commonly, a group of pads worked together in an area for general effects. Alternatively, the intensity may be gradually increased on all the pads at once to produce general movements rather than specifically in individual muscles.

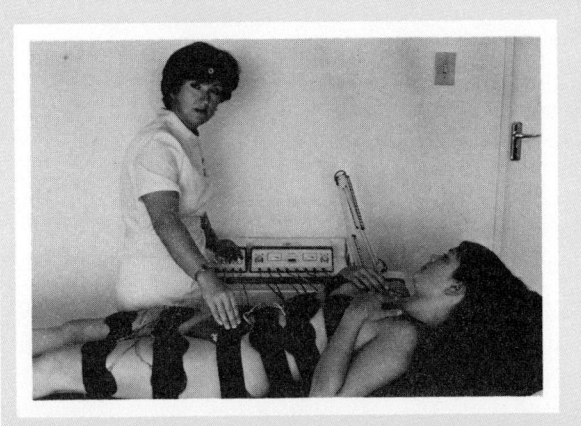

APPLYING THE CURRENT

This way of 'bringing up' or building contractions and muscle activity will depend on the area of treatment and the type of muscle it is, and how it normally works. The overall strength of the muscle is another factor to consider as is the amount of overlying fatty tissue present. Until the client becomes adjusted to the faradic treatment it may not always be possible to obtain visible contractions, often not on the first clinic visit.

Clients have to understand, however, that in order to get excellent results, their muscles have to work clearly and actively. Also, if muscle activity is obtained deep within the muscles, this will act to re-establish the tone of the muscle and help to build towards the stronger contractions needed to obtain figure shaping results.

Muscle areas can then be brought up to an active level. In the abdominal padding, this could well be applied by bringing both sets of pads placed on the rectus abdominis muscle up to a nearly active level, and then bringing up the oblique muscles, which will gain from the current transference effect, and increasing the intensity until both sets of muscles form a retraction-type of movement.

BRINGING CONTRACTIONS UP TO AN ACTIVE LEVEL

Check with the client for comfort and effect, repositioning if necessary

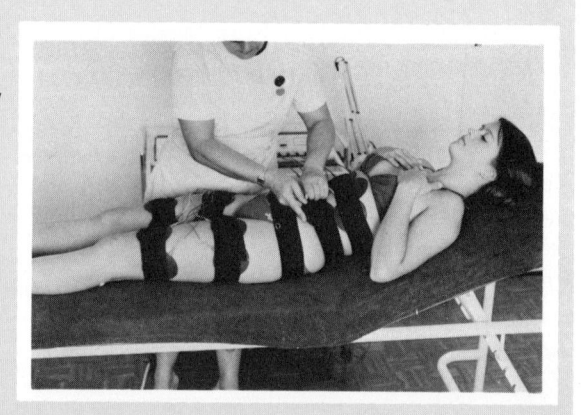

The evenness of the contractions — balance on both sides of the body — any excessive pull to one side — discomfort under a pad — stronger action under one pad or muscle area — areas not responding to the current and not forming contractions — can all be checked at this stage before the full activity/contraction level is reached, as this saves a lot of time and avoids client discomfort. Some of the unevenness experienced can relate to inadequate levels of intensity — too little current being applied — which can appear as a tremor or an unwillingness of the muscle to respond. To check this point a very small amount of extra current intensity can be applied, to see if it improves the reaction. Without an adequate amount of current, the muscle cannot contract or respond, however accurately the pad has been placed on the motor point. After applying slightly more intensity, the contractions can be watched for a few minutes to see if they balance out as the body settles into the application.

CLIENT COMFORT

Any pads actually causing discomfort, or pulling badly, should immediately be turned down to zero on their outlet connections using the colour coded leads to check that the correct pads are being dealt with. The client can guide the therapist to ensure the right pad is being altered. These offending pads can then be checked for position, wetness, firmness, and good connection on the leads, and be altered if necessary and brought back smoothly into the contraction, gradually increasing the intensity.

Discomfort is normally caused by bad positioning, but clients do also have areas of the body which prove especially sensitive to faradic applications, a fact which cannot be known prior to the application, but which must be recognized and dealt with early within treatment. If some pads seem to be causing no reaction at all, they must also be returned to zero on the control, and the leads, connections and pads checked for faults or poor preparation. Even with regular maintenance of equipment, faults can develop from constant usage, and wires can fracture inside the leads causing no current to flow, or intermittent performance if the wire is half-intact and keeps touching with movement of the lead. If either seems to be the problem, the lead will need replacement. The plastic casing around the leads and especially at the connections into the machine outlets helps to minimize this problem on the *Beauty Galley* faradic system.

More commonly the fault of current not getting through is due to the connection plug not being properly pushed into the outlet, a fact which should be checked prior to the treatment. With the connection plugs on the *Beauty Gallery* faradic system, this cannot easily occur as plugs have been chosen which push in with a firm reassuring click, this tells the operator the lead has made good contact. If no reaction is forthcoming from an area, the first thing that must be done is to turn down the intensity to zero while the problem is investigated. Otherwise the client could suddenly become connected into a high level of intensity as the connection is made or a plug pushed in.

All these initial problems of getting the routine applied well and the client settled into a comfortable application are most likely not going to occur, but if they do they have to be dealt with there and then for the routine to proceed in a satisfactory way. If not resolved, a good treatment will not result. It is worth taking a little trouble over getting the initial pad layout correct, and ensuring the client has a comfortable treatment without anxiety or discomfort.

From this careful application the operator not only learns the state of her client's muscles and their potential to respond, but most importantly gains the client's trust in her as a professional therapist. One who is not only able to apply it well but can adapt it carefully to meet individual needs.

ADJUSTING THE CURRENT

Once the client has become accustomed to the sensation of the treatment, the current may be gradually increased, and the client encouraged to relax into the muscular contractions, and not to fight them. The activity of the contractions then settles and slightly more intensity may be needed to bring them back to the ideal working level. How quickly this active level is reached, depends on the client's comfort and acceptance of the application.

The application can then be left at this active level for 15 to 20 minutes initially, even less in some cases, possibly being increased to 20 to 25 minutes on later treatments; it is not really necessary to lengthen the application, rather to increase its effectiveness. If the entire padding layout requires additional depth and intensity into the muscles, the 'depth' control can be used to increase the effect through all the pads equally. If only certain areas need an increased action, then these should be altered through individual outlet controls, to avoid applying more intensity than required to sensitive areas such as the abdomen or breasts. As the depth control provides more power into the muscles it can be used where muscles are very weak, or where the muscles are covered with a fatty layer which acts to block the current. It should not be used instead of individual controls but in addition to them, like an over-drive, when needed to make the treatment more effective and comfortable.

ADJUSTING THE CURRENT

The depth control can be used to provide extra power into the muscles, when needed

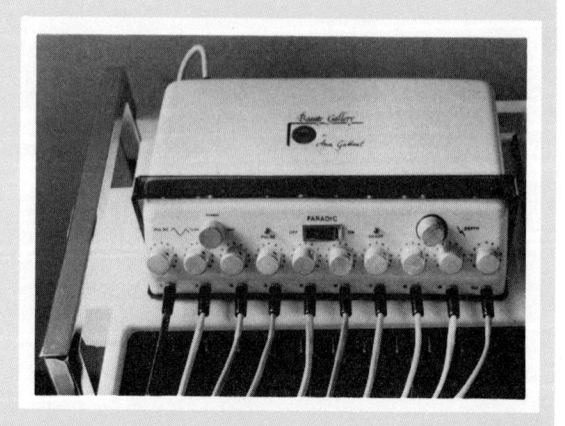

LOOKING AFTER THE CLIENT — AVOIDING MUSCLE FATIGUE

If the pads are accurately placed, specific muscle contraction is very concentrated, and long application periods only lead to muscle fatigue, with associated aching and tired muscles following treatment. Especially on initial treatments the therapist should stay with her client and encourage and reassure her about the treatment, also ensuring that active muscle contraction levels are maintained, even if the application is of quite short duration the first time. A minor treatment can always be offered to help the profitability of the routine, such as manicure, eyebrow shaping, etc., but only if the client is relaxed, warm and comfortable.

Once clients are used to having muscle toning and feel at home with the routine, several clients can be supervised at a time in individual or double cubicles, with the operator moving between them to check periodically and adjust the treatment's progression. This makes the treatment a very profitable one to offer in the clinic, and makes better use of the therapist's time. It can, however, also lead to ineffective applications or anxiety for the client, as there is the tendency to simply plug the client up and leave her, and for a large proportion of the treatment time the muscles are not working fully or to their greatest capacity, or are becoming over-treated, with fatigue going unnoticed. So new, anxious, or difficult clients should always receive the therapist's total attention, and the treatment should be costed in such a way to make this possible.

Muscle fatigue or unevenness of contractions has to be watched for within the application, and will show as a slowing down of the contraction, an unwillingness to contract actively, or spasmodic contractions. It has been seen that unevenness or pulling in one direction can occur if insufficient current is being used to initiate a muscle response, but this is in the early stages of the treatment when the muscles are adjusting to the application. Muscle fatigue occurs when the treatment has been applied for too long a period for the state of the muscles at that time. As the muscles' strength and tone improves, they are able to exercise more actively and for longer without fatigue. This is in just the same way as naturally performed exercise, but whereas in natural exercise the person would feel unable to continue to perform the exercise without pain and would stop, in artificial exercise this does not occur in the same way. The muscles are being artificially stimulated to create a contraction response, and will continue to attempt to do so well beyond their capacity to respond. This is muscle fatigue, the after-effects of which, like overdoing natural exercise, are aching muscles, pain in the area, and tiredness.

If there are signs of muscles faltering, appearing unwilling to continue active contractions, etc., when the treatment has been in action for a reasonable period — 10 minutes or more — the treatment should be concluded, if a tiny increase in current does not balance the contraction. Muscles tire very quickly when exercised so specifically by muscle toning, and this is why it can produce such excellent results, because it is so effective. Some muscles will tire more easily than others if their initial condition is weaker, and these areas can be turned off at an earlier stage in the routine, leaving other stronger areas to continue working for a longer period. The pads can remain in place but inactive, until the overall conclusion of the treatment to avoid disrupting the routine. *No area should continue to be exercised when it has become fatigued, and the fatigue must be noticed by the therapist.*

TREATMENT ADJUSTMENTS

The treatment may need periodic adjustments during the application, but once the client is used to the routine she can normally have the contractions brought to a comfortable and active level very quickly, and can stay at this level for the whole 20 to 25 minute period within the 30 minute treatment. The current intensity may need adjustment to keep the muscles at this active working level, so that full benefit is gained. It may be desirable initially to let the client get used to the treatment and its unusual sensation so that her confidence is built up and she is not anxious about the experience. But once this initial stage is over, the muscles must be made to work actively, causing clear, visible contractions if results are to be obtained. It is pointless the client having hours of treatment which do not produce the results required, and very often muscle contraction is applied ineffectively in this way through careless work, and an inability to guide the client correctly and encourage her efforts. The therapist must not be a bully, but must encourage her clients to get their muscles working, both in the clinic and at home, if they are ever to become stronger.

CONCLUDING THE ROUTINE

At the conclusion of the routine, in the same way as the contractions were 'built up', they are then reduced gradually, progressively, but at a much faster rate than when increasing the intensity. Each group of muscles can be reduced at a time, or the entire padding reduced simultaneously through the individual knobs of the outlet controls, working backwards and forwards across the machine until all knobs are at zero. This is a comfortable way to conclude the routine as it lets the muscles relax gradually after their exertion, and it only takes a moment or two to complete. If the depth control has been used within the application, this can be used to decrease all the outlets equally down to the starting point of its use. Then the individual outlet controls must be returned to zero. This leaves the system in a safe state ready for the next treatment. With all controls at zero, the machine should be switched off and the client quickly released from the straps, leads and pads. As these come off the client they must be placed back into the trolley system in sequence, leaving them ready to be cleansed and available immediately for the next client. The client can be made comfortable by drying the skin, and applying a light dusting of talc with a few seconds of soothing massage, which helps to disperse any products of fatigue in the muscles such as lactic acid — a known side-effect of muscular activity and tiredness.

The straps can remain in readiness on the bed, or be tidied ready for use, while the client is getting dressed. The pads can quickly be cleansed at the same time, while still attached to the leads, lifted out, sterilized, and replaced exactly back in order to avoid them becoming tangled together. By not making a lot of work and tidying to do, through good organization, muscle contraction treatments can be offered on a half-hourly basis, keeping the system in constant and profitable use.

TREATMENT PLANNING AND ORGANIZATION

To be really effective for figure shaping, muscle toning has to be applied at least three times a week, for half-hour sessions. These can either form the basis of the figure treatment course on their own, offered as a course or programme of muscle toning, or they can be a part of an overall slimming/reduction plan and be associated with other forms of body treatment, such as pre-heating, vacuum massage, manual work, vibratory massage or galvanic treatments for cellulite, all of which are backed by a reduction diet. In either case, the muscle toning needs to be applied regularly to be effective, even when reinforced by home exercise efforts. It has a progressive effect on the muscle tone and strength, and this is considerably improved if treatment is given in quick succession.

Treatment can be given each day, because it is not an unnatural action for the body but one that strengthens its own physical resources. See *Beauty Guide 2, Figure Treatment,* by Ann Gallant, for further information on treatment planning and building a body service.

ENCOURAGING THE CLIENT'S OWN EFFORTS

When the client has just completed the muscle contraction treatment and her muscles feel strong, it is a very good time to get her to practise her own exercises, while the 'imprint' of the artificial stimulation remains on the nerve path. Clients will find it so much easier to obtain and hold a contraction at this time, that they become very encouraged in their personal efforts at home. Once they are aware their muscles can hold them in firmly without strain or too much conscious effort, it makes them aware of their own physical potential. Isometric contractions can be used to help this re-education process, holding in the abdominal muscles, lifting upwards and with shoulders back to flatten the abdomen and tighten the waist, and clenching the buttocks and inside thigh areas to firm these softer areas as well.

Active exercise can be used as well, toe touching, waist rotation, arm swinging, etc., all possible so much more easily when the muscles are supple and working well, responding correctly to the nervous stimulus, even if initially it is applied artificially. (See *Body Treatments and Dietetics for the Beauty Therapist,* by Ann Gallant, for more exercise information.)

Muscle contraction acts to train the muscles back into correct functioning, and is in this way an excellent treatment. Clients rediscover their muscles, and even if they never can or will complete natural exercise really successfully, they will be able to keep in good condition with regular passive exercise.

Courses of treatment are normally offered running over an 8 to 10 week period, so that if a weight loss is involved, it has time to take effect. Many treatment courses are presented so that muscle toning is included 3 times a week, and on one or two of these treatments the routine would include other aspects such as galvanic treatments for cellulite, vibratory massage, vacuum suction, etc., to help speed overall reduction.

Muscle contraction for body shaping and firming is one of the most popular treatments the clinic has to offer. It is also one of the most profitable, and many slimming clinics are based primarily on muscle toning in a range of different forms. Few systems of treatment have such a wide range of applications, or are as effective in gaining results as muscle contraction. With efficient application it is the greatest earning system of body therapy available, and because of the excellent results obtained is well liked by clients.

If a clinic specializes in body therapy with the emphasis on muscle toning routines, it is possible to operate several cubicles for treatment with just a couple of well trained therapists. If careful client

ENCOURAGING THE CLIENT

(a)

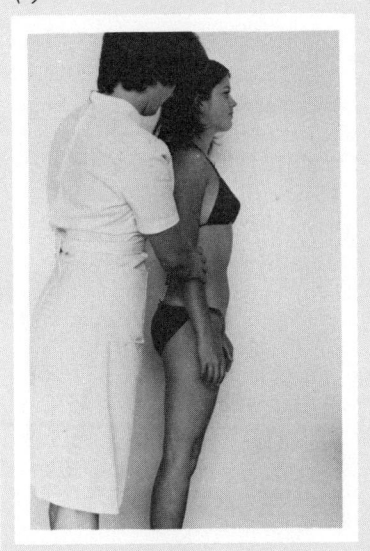

(a), (b) Check the client's posture — so she can relate to how she should feel and move when her muscles are strong, and holding her firmly

(b)

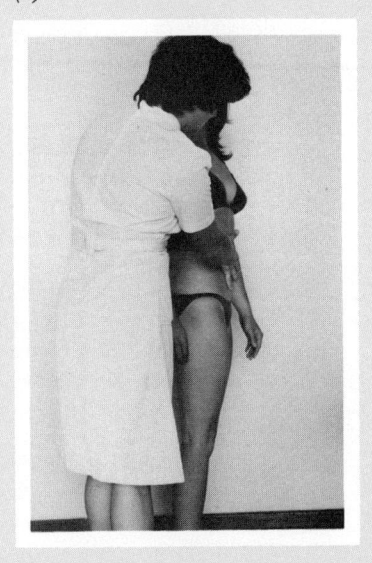

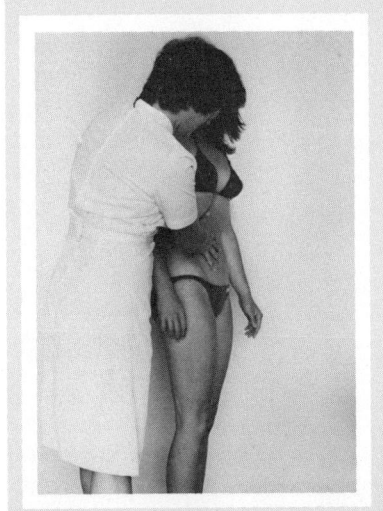

(c) Encourage the client's exercise efforts when the 'imprint' of the muscle toning can still be felt on the muscles, guiding the client to concentrate specifically on one area at a time

records are kept, and weighing, measuring, etc., is undertaken regularly, a large flow of clients can easily be dealt with, while still retaining a personal approach. Good organization and well equipped facilities make this possible, and it is a method that is very popular in city clinics where the flow of clients is large.

No other system of body therapy earns its keep as effectively as muscle contraction, and it has established itself as the most important element in slimming treatments.

MUSCLE TONING CHECK LIST — REASONS FOR POOR OR UNEVEN CONTRACTIONS

(1) Poor skin preparation — skin not clean, oil in the skin, etc.
(2) Inaccurate placing of the pads on to motor points.
(3) Lack of moisture on the pads' surface — pads drying out, being dirty, etc., which could cause a tissue burn, known as a faradic burn.
(4) Insufficient intensity of current to initiate a muscular response.
(5) Slack strapping causing poor skin contact, skin irritation, etc., poor current flow.
(6) Loose or faulty connections, giving intermittent performance.
(7) Excessive weight deposits acting as block or barrier to the electrical flow.
(8) Insufficient pads applied for the task or area to be exercised.
(9) Picking up unwanted muscle actions or joint actions due to placing pads too close to muscle origins or insertions (bone attachments of muscles).
(10) Uneven contractions caused by differences in both sides of the body, which can be accommodated by using split body paddings and balancing intensities.
(11) Greater skin resistance under one of the pads.
(12) Pads not placed on identical areas of muscle bulk either side of the body, or placed slightly higher or lower in relation to the midline of the body.

7

Facial faradism

ADVANTAGES OF FACIAL EXERCISE

The facial and neck muscles can be exercised comfortably with the facial applicator/electrode available as an optional accessory on the faradic system of the *Beauty Gallery*.

Facial exercise can help maintain the muscles' good tone, and is useful to prevent or delay the formation of wrinkles, fine lines, crepy skin or atrophic ageing conditions. Like muscle toning of the body, facial faradism works in a natural way to keep the facial contours firm, and avoid early signs of ageing, loss of taut skin texture, slackness in the neck tissues, crepiness and bags under the eyes, etc.

For facial exercise, the applicator works from one outlet, and is controlled by its intensity control knob. The machine is switched on and the 'pulse' set to normal or fast, according to which proves most comfortable for the client. The depth control is not needed, as the outlet has adequate power for the small facial muscles involved, and so must be left at zero.

The facial applicator provides stimulation of closely-positioned facial muscles through the two active conductive discs on its working surface. Due to the tiny nature and close inter-relationship of facial muscles, the active discs which stimulate the muscles have to be close to each other on the applicator. This avoids involving unwanted areas or muscles in the chosen facial movement, which could cause facial distortion or discomfort. The polarity of the two active disc electrodes alternates in the same way as the body pads, and both discs must be moist and in firm skin contact in order to initiate a muscular response.

CONTRA-INDICATIONS TO FACIAL FARADISM

There are very few contra-indications to facial exercise as it is a very natural process when applied well. Cuts or surface abrasions, open spots, or skin infections are, however, contra-indications.

If the client has hypersensitive skin, or is of a nervous disposition, it should be applied very carefully, letting the client adjust to the sensation gently. If the client suffers from migraine headaches it should not be used on the forehead area, and initially treatments should be restricted to one or two contractions per muscle to see that the client does not get an adverse reaction to the artificial exercise.

A lot of fillings in the teeth requires adaptation of the application to avoid toothache occurring, but does not prevent treatment overall.

The presence of widespread dilated capillaries on the cheeks also limits the application, but does not necessarily contra-indicate it altogether.

If the client has a medical history involving Bell's palsy, or has had a stroke or thrombosis in the past, medical guidance should be sought and permission obtained prior to application of the facial exercise.

APPLICATION OF FACIAL EXERCISE

The facial exerciser is applied to a clean skin which is moistened, and carefully positioned to be on an active motor point or nerve source. The discs of the applicator must be kept moist at all times by constant re-wetting, otherwise good reactions will not result. The primary sensation is stimulation of sensory or surface nerves under the contact area of the applicator, causing slight skin prickling, and skin reddening (erythema) in the area. If the applicator is accurately placed, when sufficient intensity of current is applied, muscle contractions take place (normally intensity level 4 to 7 on the faradic system of the *Beauty Gallery*). The client should be encouraged to guide the therapist as to feeling, and to give feedback as to comfort, closeness to the muscle reaction, etc.

The surging of the current produces relaxation of the contractions, causing them to be pulsed. Exercise should be given at a comfortable level, causing activity in the muscles, not fierce actions or facial distortion. The purpose of working the muscles is to tone them naturally, which exerts a pumping effect on blood and lymphatic vessels in the area, improving general circulation and elimination. This brings about an interchange of tissue fluids and increased nutrition to the skin's surface, helping it to retain a youthful appearance. Most clients feel the treatment keeps their contours firm, and their skin full of vigour.

FACIAL EXERCISE SEQUENCE OF APPLICATION

Each facial area to be exercised can be worked in sequence, with 6 to 8 contractions only needed on each area. The treatment can be applied very quickly once experience grows in placing the facial applicator accurately, and should not take more than 10 minutes to apply.

The muscle exercise sequence is:
(1) sterno mastoid
(2) platysma
(3) masseter
(4) superficial cheek
(5) risorius
(6) zygomaticus
(7) orbicularis oris
(8) orbicularis oculi
(9) frontalis (if not contra-indicated).

Each area should be worked in sequence, starting with the neck by working on both sides of the neck on the sterno mastoid muscles, followed by three positions on the fascia-type platysma muscle covering the throat, each side and under the point of the jaw.

The masseter muscle follows, exercised in two alternate positions, one along the mandible (jawbone), pushing upwards, and the other in front of the ear where the facial nerve enters the cheek, and here the applicator is used in a horizontal position, pushing towards the mouth.

The superficial cheek muscles are treated next, either from the facial nerve position, which affects the entire cheek, eye and lip area, or exercised separately. When worked individually the muscles treated first are the risorius, which pulls the mouth outwards into a grin, then the zygomaticus which lifts the corner of the mouth upwards, and then the orbicularis oris which firms and tightens the sphincter muscle of the mouth.

The eye area can then be exercised gently by placing the applicator on positions on the angle of the upper cheek bone, and at the side of the eye, to work the orbicularis oculi. This is another sphincter muscle (a muscle which closes on itself and has no bony attachments, but attaches into the fascia of other muscles), and only needs a small amount of current to tighten the eye skin and cause activity in the area.

The forehead can be exercised, if it is not uncomfortable for the client, by working the frontalis muscle, from a position on the inside area of the eyebrow. This causes the eyebrow to lift, and eases out heavy vertical lines between the brows, and also helps superficial flexure lines. If the treatment is uncomfortable it is contra-indicated in this area.

FACIAL MUSCLE EXERCISE

(a) Working position, client semi-reclining, facial muscles in a natural position, therapist able to control the application and current intensity on faradic unit

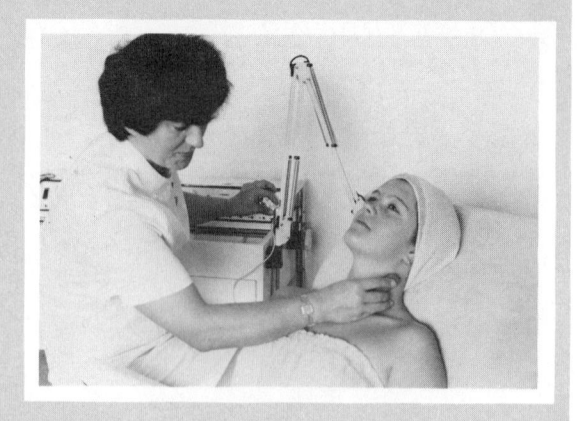

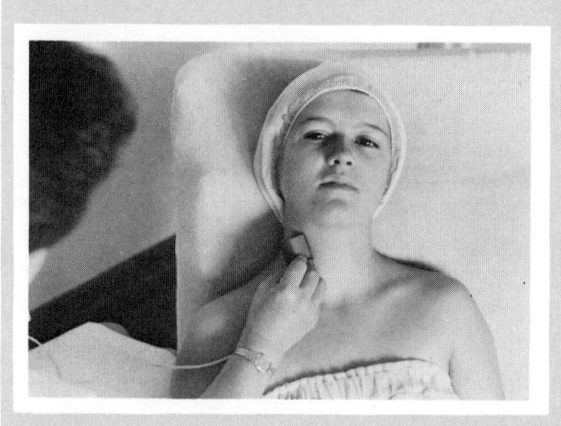

(b) The sterno mastoid muscle is exercised for 6 to 8 contractions on each side of the neck

(c) The client can guide the application, providing essential feedback to the therapist

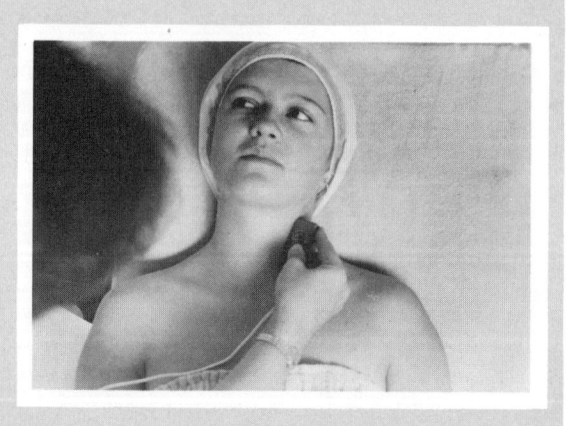

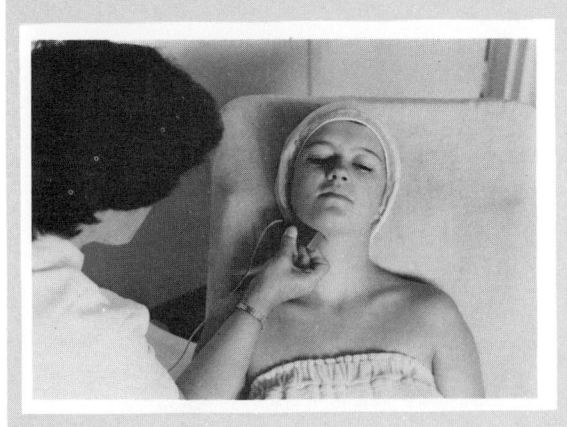

(d) The platysma muscle — 3 positions on this fascia (sheet-like) muscle which attaches into other muscles of the jawline and upper chest

(e) Either side of the point of the jaw, with the applicator angled towards the chin. The muscle action lifts the skin of the neck upwards

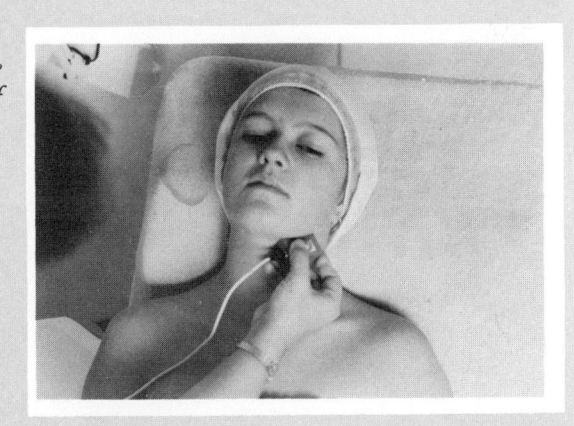

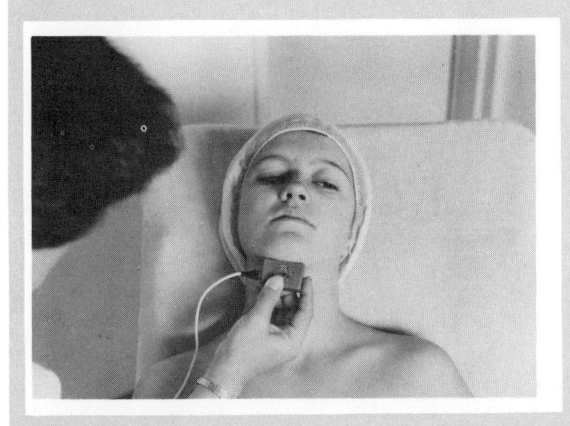

(f) Under the chin, pushed forwards, the action causes the chin to firm, crinkling the skin, while under the jaw the muscle is tightened, helping to prevent a double chin

(g) The masseter muscle which works either from positions in front of the ears

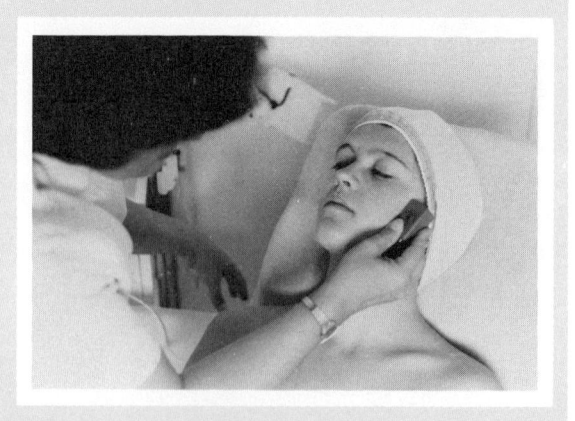

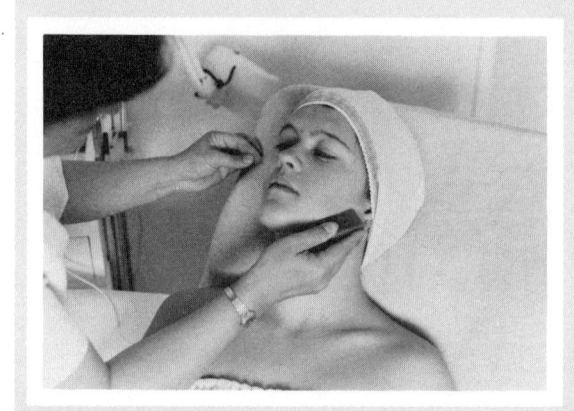

(h) or close to its deep attachments on the mandible (lower jaw)

(i) Its action is to clench the jaw and firm the profile

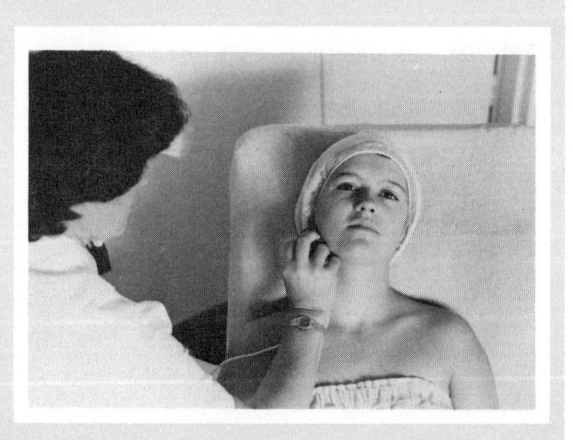

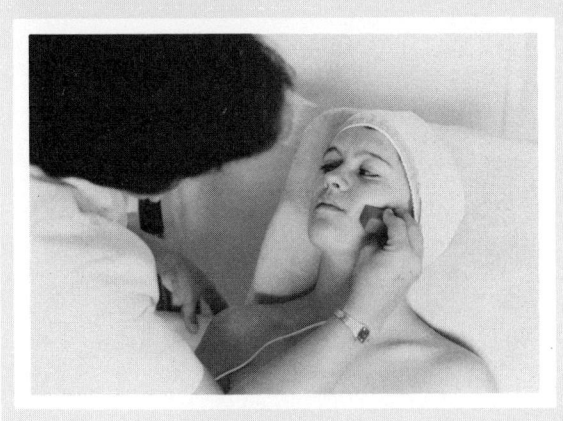

(j) The superficial cheek muscles, the risorius (which also exercise the orbicularis oris by muscle connection). All the superficial muscles of the face can be exercised by the facial nerve

(k) The zygomaticus muscle, which affects the cheek and lip

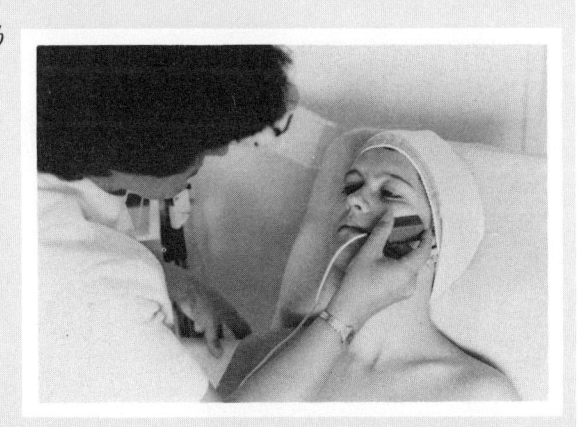

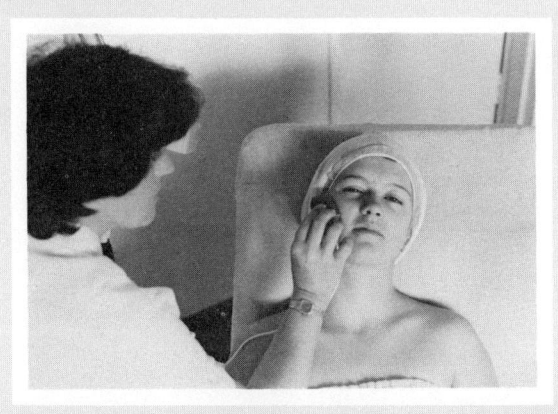

(l) The zygomaticus also affects the eye by connection of its muscle fibres

(m) The facial nerve can be activated in front of the ear, where it enters the cheek, and will affect all surface muscles of the face. This position is very specific, as it is the trunk of the nerve, from which branches radiate to other areas

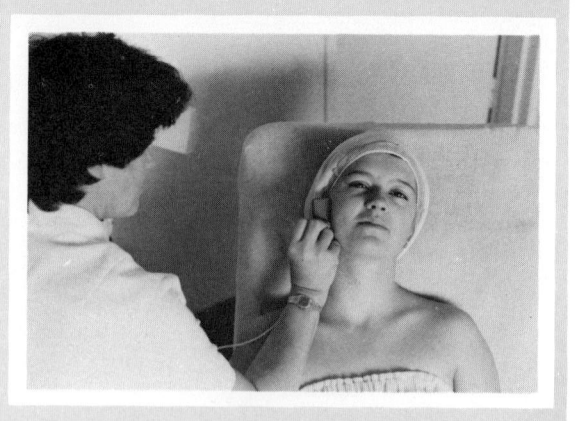

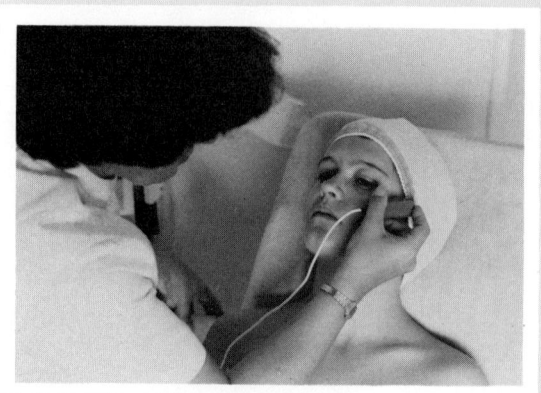

(n) The orbicularis oculi can be treated separately to exercise the upper and lower lids and so improve skin texture and muscle tone

(o) The eye should not be forced to close by the contraction, but rather be exercised with a gentle action

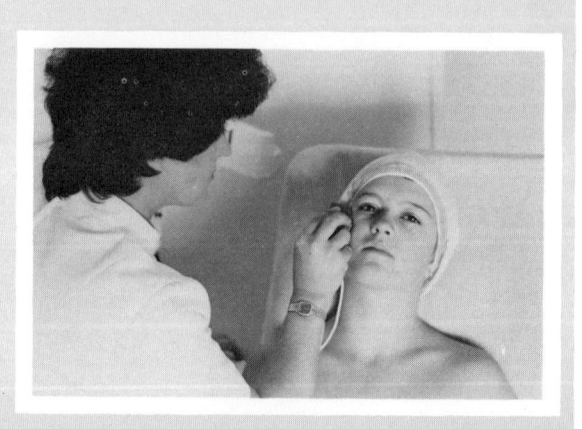

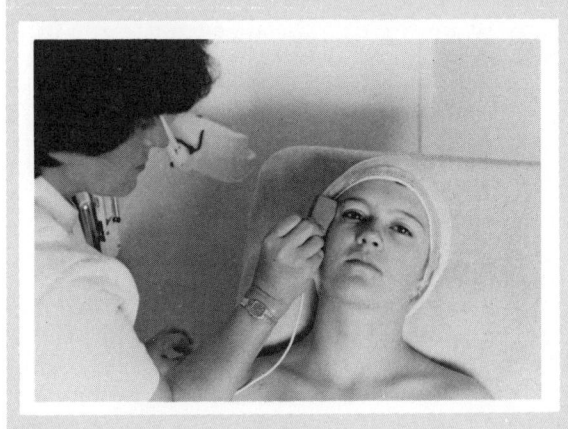

(p) The orbicularis oculi may also be exercised from an upper position which helps the upper lid and eyebrow area more

(q) Working in this position helps to keep the eyelid and brow skin from becoming crepy and lined

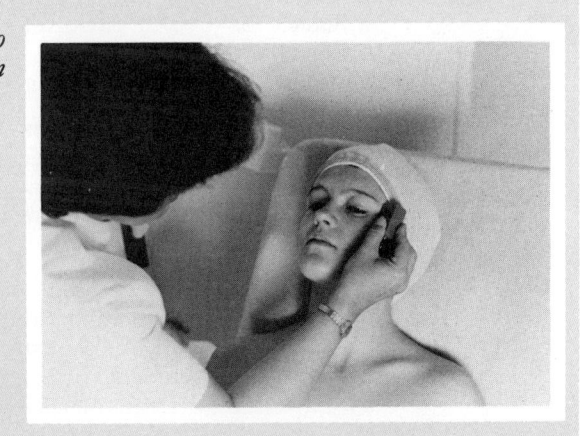

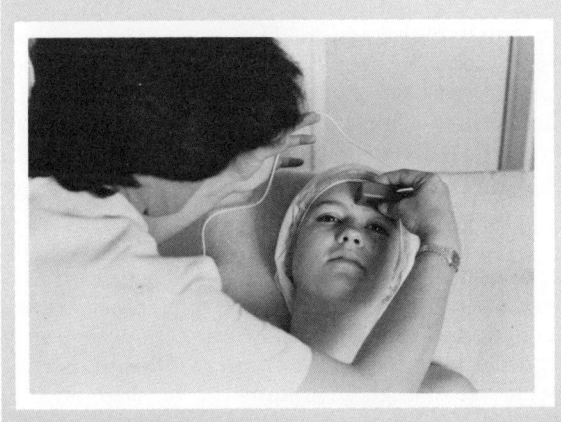

(r) The frontalis muscle can be worked if not contra-indicated through discomfort. It lifts the eyebrows and pulls the scalp forwards in the action

These main positions for muscle exercise are adequate and firm the contours of the face and neck, delaying the softening effect around the eyes caused by fine lining and crepy skin texture. Treatment can be adapted if one area of the face needs special attention.

ADAPTING THE TREATMENT

If the client has a lot of fillings in the teeth, or wears dentures with metal bridge work, then the muscle of the mouth — the orbicularis oris — can be exercised indirectly by working the facial nerve position, at the point where it enters the superficial cheek in front of the ear. Or, the muscle can be worked through its connection into the risorius, by working that muscle and indirectly affecting the mouth through muscular connection.

The eye area only needs a pulsing activity surging through it, which causes the skin to flutter and ripple and the area to become suffused with energy. This refreshes the eyes and helps avoid puffiness, fine lining, dark shadows and bags under the eyes.

Unnatural contractions are unnecessary and do not help the facial profile in any way. For this reason the triangularis muscle which depresses the corner of the lower lip is not treated, as it pulls the face into an unattractive grimace, which feels uncomfortable to the client.

As it is evident that people who use their facial muscles in an expressive and active way tend to obtain more, rather than fewer facial lines, it is obvious that strong facial exercises are not really desirable. It is preferable instead to activate the muscles working at a level where the small muscles contract in much the same way as an isometric exercise, that is contracting and firming without too much movement at their bony attachments. Many facial muscles have no bony attachments, but insert or attach to other muscles, and so contracting one muscle often causes several others to become involved in the exercise action. That is why the positive and negative alternating polarity discs on the facial applicator have to be so small and close together. Any larger or further apart, and it would be almost impossible to treat a facial muscle in isolation to get a clear movement.

GETTING RID OF UNWANTED ACTIONS

If the muscle responds in a fierce or unpleasant action, these unwanted effects can be lost by first decreasing the intensity level of the current applied, and then carefully repositioning more accurately on the muscle, with special attention to its motor point. Sometimes a slight change of angle in holding the facial applicator is sufficient to correct the action, and bring clear and comfortable contractions. The intensity level is increased gradually until this occurs, with the client providing guidance as to the accuracy of the position, its comfort, etc., and how close to the correct position it is on the muscle. The client feels the response occurring before the therapist can see or feel it through the skin, and it is correct procedure to involve her in the treatment.

WHERE TO APPLY MUSCLE EXERCISE

The facial exercise is normally applied at the conclusion of a facial treatment when the skin is clean, moist and relaxed, and likely to respond well to the faradic-type current, thus minimizing primary skin prickling. It can, however, be applied at any stage of treatment when the skin is clean, free from oils, etc.

For effective results, if the client has a skin tone problem with slackness in facial and neck muscles, the treatment should ideally be given several times weekly, and can be applied independently of facial therapy. If clients are on a reduction plan and losing weight steadily, it could be applied following the body muscle toning, to prevent skin slackness occurring on the facial area. It is up to the therapist to advise her client of the advantages of toning both her face and body together, for the therapist is aware of the unattractive results that can occur to the skin when a person loses weight, and her client may be unaware of the problem until it happens. The therapist must provide a total caring service, and guide her clients with professional skill and integrity, letting them know what is available to help them look good, and feel fit.

Useful Addresses

PROFESSIONAL ORGANIZATIONS AND EXAMINATION BOARDS

Further information on courses is available from the following examination boards and professional organizations:

Aestheticians' International Association Inc,
5206 McKinney, Dallas, Texas, USA

American Electrolysis Association,
Corresponding Secretary Sandi Strum, 211 Jonnet Building, 4099 William Penn Highway, Monroeville P.A. 15146, USA

Beauty Education International — Beauty Club
Ann Gallant, Forum, Stirling Road, Chichester PO19 2EN, UK

E A Ellison & Co Ltd, Brindley Road South, Exhall, Coventry CV7 9EP, UK

Esthetic and Beauty Supply, 16 Coldwater Road, Don Mills, Ontario M3B 1Y7, Canada Tel (416) 444 1154
There is also a Californian office, USA

British Association of Beauty Therapy and Cosmetology,
Secretary Mrs D. Parkes, Suite 5, Wolesley House, Oriel Road, Cheltenham GL50 1TH, UK

British Association of Electrolysis,
16 Quakers Mead, Haddenham, Bucks HP17 8EB, UK

British Biosthetic Society,
2 Birkdale Drive, Bury, Greater Manchester BL8 2SG, UK

City and Guilds of London Institute,
46 Britannia Street, London WC1 9RG, UK

Le Comité Internationale D'Esthétiques et de Cosmetologie, (CIDESCO),
CIDESCO International Secretariat, PO Box 9, A1095 Vienna, Austria

Confederation of Beauty Therapy and Cosmetology,
Education Secretary Mrs B. Longhurst, 3 The Retreat, Lidwells Lane, Goudhurst, Kent, UK

Institute of Electrolysis,
251 Seymour Grove, Manchester M16 0DS, UK

International Aestheticians' Association,
2304 Monument Boulevard, Pleasant Hill, California 94523, USA

National Federation of Health and Beauty Therapists,
PO Box 36, Arundel, West Sussex BN18 0SW, UK

International Therapy Examination Council,
3 The Planes, Bridge Road, Chertsey, Surrey KT16 8LE, UK

The Northern Institute of Massage,
100 Waterloo Road, Blackpool FY4 1AW, UK

Skin Care Association of America,
16 West 57th Street, New York, NY, USA

South African Institute of Health and Beauty Therapists,
PO Box 56318, Pinegowrie 2123, South Africa

EQUIPMENT MANUFACTURERS

Ann Gallant Beauté Therapy Equipment,
Esthetic and Beauty Supply, 16 Coldwater Road, Don Mills,
Ontario M3B 1Y7, Canada, Tel (416) 444 1154
There is also a Californian office, USA

Beauty Gallery Equipment by Ann Gallant,
E. A. Ellison & Co Ltd, Brindley Road South,
Exhall, Coventry CV7 9EP, UK, Tel (0203) 362505

Colne Development Co Ltd,
2 Station Road, Twickenham, Middlesex, UK

Cristal (Equipment),
86 Rue Pixérécourt, 75020 Paris, France

Depilex Ltd and Slimaster Beauty Equipment Ltd,
Regent House, Dock Road, Birkenhead, Merseyside L41 1DG,
UK

Electro-Medical Services,
Bermuda Road, Nuneaton, Warks, UK

George Solly Organization Ltd,
James House, Queen Street, Henley on Thames, Oxon, UK

Soltron Solarium and Sun Beds,
Josef Kratz, Vertriebsgesellschaft mbH Rottbitzer Straße
69-5340 Bad Honnef 6 Tel 02224/818-0 Telex jk 8861194

Nemectron Belmont Inc,
17 West 56th Street, New York, NY10019, USA

Silhouette International Beauty Equipment,
Kenwood Road, Reddish, Stockport, Cheshire SK5 6PH, UK

Slendertone Ltd,
12-14 Baker Street, London W1M 2HA, UK

Taylor Reeson Ltd,
96-98 Dominion Road, Worthing, Sussex, UK

TREATMENT PRODUCT SUPPLIERS

Ann Gallant Beauté Therapy Products,
Esthetic and Beauty Supply, 16 Coldwater Road, Don Mills,
Ontario M3B 1Y7, Canada
There is also a Californian office, USA

Elizabeth of Schwarzenberg,
13 Windsor Street, Chertsey, Surrey KT16 8AY, UK

Clarins (UK) Ltd,
(Oils and body products)
150 High Street, Stratford, London E15 2NE, UK

Gallery Line by Ann Gallant, Skin Care and Body Products,
E. A. Ellison & Co Ltd, Brindley Road South,
Exhall, Coventry CV7 9EP, UK

Pier Augé Cosmetics,
Harbourne Marketing Associates, Oak House,
271 Kingston Road, Leatherhead, Surrey, UK

Thalgo Cosmetic/Importex,
(Marine based products)
5 Tristan Square, Blackheath, London SE3 9UB, UK

MAGAZINES AND TRADE PUBLICATIONS

Beauty Club by Ann Gallant
(International club for all those involved in the beauty industry —
publications/fact sheets/guides/books, etc.)

Details from:
Beauty Education International, Forum, Stirling Road,
Chichester PO19 2EN, UK
Telex 86402, CHITYP G. Ref GALLANT

Ellison, Brindley Road South, Exhall Trading Estate,
Exhall, Coventry, UK Tel 0203 362505

Esthetic and Beauty Supply, 16 Coldwater Road, Don Mills,
Ontario M3B 1Y7, Canada Tel (416) 444 1154
There is also a Californian office, USA

Health and Beauty Salon Magazine

Hair and Beauty Magazine

Hairdresser's Journal

Trade publications for the Hair and Beauty Industries, details from International Business Press, Quadrant House, The Quadrant, Sutton, Surrey, UK
(Health and Beauty Salon Magazine Editor — Ms Marion Mathews) Tel 01 661 3500

Skin Care Magazine
The National Journal of Esthetics
140 Main Street, El Segundo, California 90245, USA

Cosmetics Magazine
Specialist magazine for all those involved with the sales of cosmetics, toiletries, make-up, skin and nail care etc.
Beauty Industries Publications Ltd, Suite 201, 801 York Mills Road, Don Mills, Ontario, Canada

International Hair and Beauty Route
Specialist Magazine for Electrologists, Skin Care and Esthetics, Beauty Therapists, Editor Mr. D. Copperthwaite
PO Box 313, Port Credit Postal Station, Mississauga, Ontario, Canada

EQUIPMENT DESIGN AND DEVELOPMENT

Beauty Educational International
Design and Development of Equipment/Clinic Planning/ Market Research in the Industry

Ann Gallant
Forum, Stirling Road, Chichester PO19 2EN, UK
Telex 86402, CHITYP. G, Ref Gallant

Ellison, Brindley Road South, Exhall Trading Estate, Exhall, Coventry, UK Tel (0203) 362505

Esthetic and Beauty Supply, 16 Coldwater Road, Don Mills, Ontario M3B 1Y7, Canada Tel (416) 444 1154
There is also a Californian office, USA

A NOTE ON BEAUTY EDUCATION INTERNATIONAL — BEAUTY CLUB

Beauty Club offers a unique service to the beauty industry; through COMMUNICATION, MOTIVATION and EDUCATION the club can provide all the necessary information for success in this exciting and profitable field; through its own Newsletter it keeps its members informed of all the latest developments in the industry around the world.

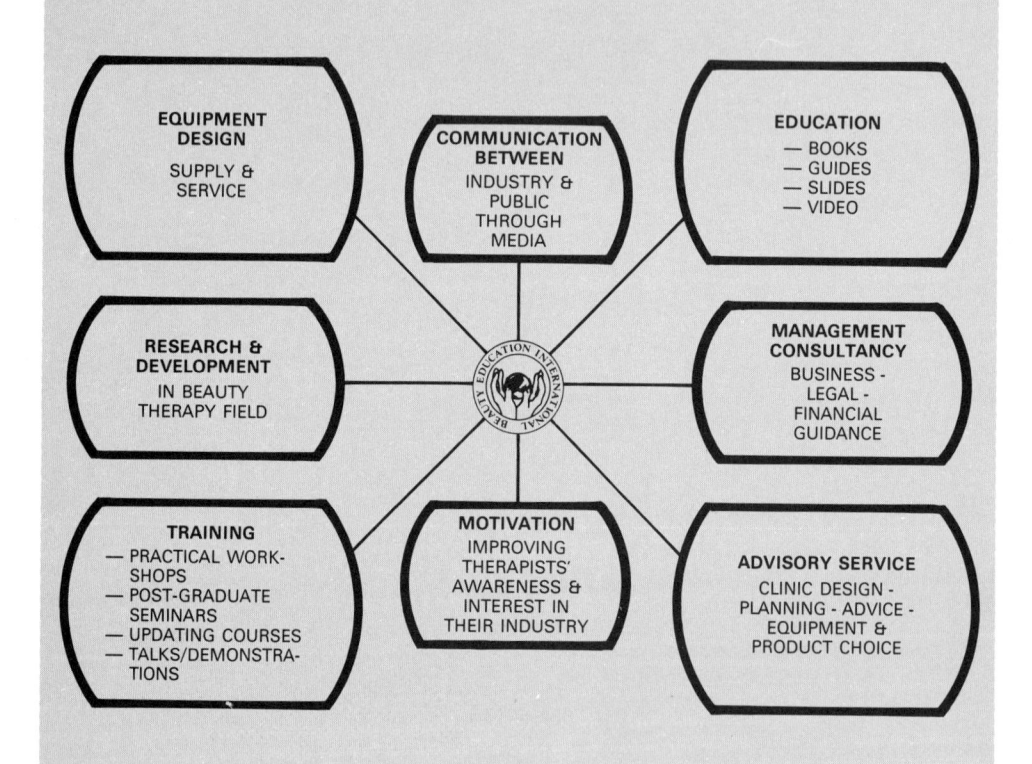

EQUIPMENT DESIGN
SUPPLY & SERVICE

COMMUNICATION BETWEEN
INDUSTRY & PUBLIC THROUGH MEDIA

EDUCATION
— BOOKS
— GUIDES
— SLIDES
— VIDEO

RESEARCH & DEVELOPMENT
IN BEAUTY THERAPY FIELD

MANAGEMENT CONSULTANCY
BUSINESS - LEGAL - FINANCIAL GUIDANCE

TRAINING
— PRACTICAL WORKSHOPS
— POST-GRADUATE SEMINARS
— UPDATING COURSES
— TALKS/DEMONSTRATIONS

MOTIVATION
IMPROVING THERAPISTS' AWARENESS & INTEREST IN THEIR INDUSTRY

ADVISORY SERVICE
CLINIC DESIGN - PLANNING - ADVICE - EQUIPMENT & PRODUCT CHOICE

WHAT MEMBERSHIP OF BEAUTY CLUB CAN OFFER

★ A feeling of belonging to a truly international club.

★ Regular Beauty Club Newsletters to support this linked-in club feeling.

★ The right to wear the Beauty Club Badge which shows your interest in the beauty world.

★ Beauty Club Member's Card for preferential buying terms and discounts on a selected range of salon equipment and products.

★ Information and expertise from leading experts in the field.

★ News of latest advances in the industry.

★ Technical fact sheets for easy reference on products, equipment and treatment systems, etc.

★ Guidance and practical support on retailing products for home use.

★ A link into Beauty Education International for:
Books, Beauty Guides, Technical Information, Research and Development Programmes, Clinic Planning Guidance, Stock Management.

★ Training — practical workshops, post graduate seminars, up-dating courses, talks/demonstrations.

★ Motivation — improving therapists' awareness and interest in their industry.

Anyone who is interested in the beauty industry, and wants to keep up to date and in touch with the latest knowledge and techniques available to help them in their work is eligible to join.

ANN GALLANT
Int. B. Th. Dip. D.R.E.